Old Foye Days

Henry Noel Shore Teignmouth (baron)

FOWEY, FROM BODENICK.

From a Drawing by Wm. Daniell, in 1824.

OLD

FOYE

DAYS,

BEING

The True Story of a Cornish Haven,

COMPILED FROM VARIOUS SOURCES

BY

COMMANDER HON. HENRY N. SHORE, R.N.,

AUTHOR OF

" The Flight of the Lapwing."
" How Glasgow Ceased to Flourish."
" Smuggling Days and Smuggling Ways."

———

With numerous Illustrations by the Author.

———

" The true men of progress are those who profess as their starting point a profound respect for the past."—*Renan.*

1896.

PREFACE.

This little work is in no sense a guide-book. It was compiled in the hope of attracting increased attention to the many interesting historical associations of the town and neighbourhood.

The illustrations are an attempt to perpetuate the more picturesque aspects of the town as it was before the modern epidemic of "improvement" set in.

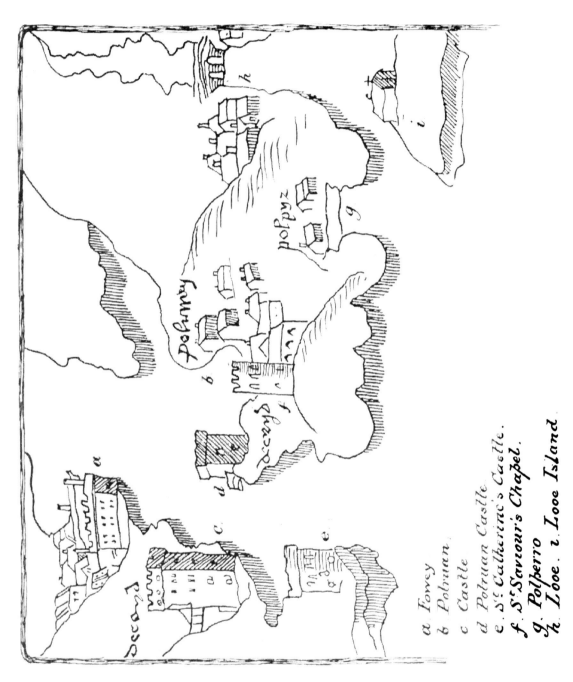

a. Fowey
b. Polruan
c. Castle
d. Polruan Castle
e. St Catherine's Castle.
f. St Saviour's Chapel.
g. Polperro
h. Looe. i. Looe Island.

FROM AN OLD CHART, TIME OF HENRY VIII.

LIST OF ILLUSTRATIONS.

PART I.

PART II.

"All that now delights thee, from the day on which it should be touched, shall melt and melt away."—*Wordsworth*.

———

PART I.

———

OLD FOYE DAYS.

CONTAINING

An Historical Sketch of the Rise, Glory, and Decline of this most Ancient Port;

TOGETHER WITH

Many curious Particulars relating to Past and Present Times,

AS WELL AS

The Manners and Customs of the Inhabitants

CONTENTS.

ERRATA.

Page 22, line 22, for *chez luis* read *chez eux*.

OLD HOUSE AT THE TOP OF FORE STREET.

OLD FOYE DAYS.

→ Chapter I. ←

The Remote Past.

LD Leland's description of this quaint little spot, although penned some three hundred years ago, is by no means inapplicable to the town at the present day. He says: " It is set on the north side of the haven, lying along the shore, and builded on the side of a great slatey, rokked hille." The place has of course expanded considerably beyond the " quarter-mile " limit of his day, and, but for the " rokked hille " which nature has set here, would doubtless have spread still further afield ; but it still preserves much of the quaint originality of former days. The streets, for example, are not like the stiff commonplace thoroughfares of most British towns : there is an individuality about them, which, though in some respects trying to the temper of the modern Jehu, delights all true lovers of the picturesque. And, then, curious old bits of architecture crop out at every turn, reminding the passer-by of those far-off times, when the haven " was haunted with shippes of diverse nations, and their shippes went to all nations "—the golden age of Fowey. You cannot, indeed, spend many hours in Fowey without feeling that it is a place with a history : every feature of it bears the impress of the past. The very stones at your feet " do the same tale repeat : " as Sir Walter Scott said of the stones of Iona, " you never tread upon them but you set your feet upon some ancient history." Not that the position in which you now find them, is the one they have always occupied, for many, which shared in the rise and fall of mansions long since vanished from the scene, have been degraded from their high estate and turned to base uses. Were these stones but endowed with the power of speech and memory what strange tales they would unfold, of the many generations of Foyens who have trod these streets since the town first sprang into life.

And yet, as a graceful and accomplished authoress has said, " Despite all the charms lent to it by Nature, the place must be wanting in real interest if it has no human associations, no tale of human joy and sorrow connected with its name, no ancient legend to give a pathos to rippling river and woodland glade : "Man is the sun of his world," and we will find it almost invariably the case that Nature's fairest scenes fail to inspire us with true interest if we cannot read upon them some human record, and connect them with the story of some toiling struggling human beings like ourselves."   The history of Fowey will be found lacking in none of these essentials, for, in olden times it was a town of no mean repute, and, little as the fact may be realised by modern English-men, its inhabitants played a part in our nation's history which may well excite the envy of dwellers in the mushroom cities that have sprung up within the last few centuries.   The Foyens of modern times may point with justifiable pride to the old chronicles which tell ot " the glorie of Fowey," and how, when the siege of Calais, in Edward III's. reign, necessitated a call for ships and mariners, their town furnished more vessels than any port in the Kingdom, and more men than any except Yarmouth.   While, in later times, the merchant-princes of Fowey did yeomen's service in laying the foundation of the world-wide commerce which has so marvellously enriched the realm.

Traces of these days of commercial prosperity may, even now, be discerned by the curious, in many parts of the town, while panelled rooms, carved stones cropping out of modern walls, fireplaces with quaint Dutch tiles, and other relics of a time when, according to modern teaching, sound and honest work were more highly esteemed than the pretentious abortions of the jerry-builder, bespeak the taste and wealth of former occupants.

It was scarcely likely that the advantages and facilities of access of the port of Fowey should have escaped the notice of the daring navigators who frequented these coasts in ancient days. There is ample evidence, indeed, to show that the haven was resorted to in very early times. That the Phœnicians came to Cornwall for its tin is well-known, and, moreover, that this intercourse with strangers had a beneficial effect on the inhabitants of the county is proved by a passage in Cæsar's Commentaries, to the effect that " the Britons of Cornwall were very hospitable, and the trade they carried on with foreign merchants had softened their manners "—a pleasing trait of character which seems somewhat unaccountably to have escaped the notice of later historians, for, we find an eminent engineer, who visited this corner of England in the latter half of last century, meeting with such rough entertainment that, in a moment of pique, forgetful of Cæsar's certificate of character, he described the Cornish as having the most disagreeable manners of any people he had ever met ! It is just possible, that if Cæsar had fallen into the hands of the wreckers of later times, he might have seen fit to modify his opinions ! The deterioration of manners which afterwards set in would form an interesting subject of inquiry.

In one respect, at least, we moderns have reason to look back with gratitude to the visits of the old Phœnician traders. For did they not initiate the Cornish into the mysteries connected with the manufacture of "clotted cream" ? Such, at any rate, we are assured is the true origin of Cornish Cream, and we are further informed by the erudite in such matters, that this now popular way of "treating" cream—how nicely these savants express their ideas— is still observed in Phœnician lands, as, for instance, about Tyre and Carthage. Now, seeing that this doctrine was expounded from a Cornish pulpit, at evensong, there can be no reason to doubt its orthodoxy.

That Fowey was much frequented by foreign shipping in remote times is a well-authenticated fact ; indeed, there is evidence to show that a Roman Colony existed here in Vespasian's time, in proof of which may be cited the discovery of coins, pottery, and stone coffins, to say nothing of certain local names which have been traced to a Roman origin. Strange that these grim old warriors and industrious road makers should have left so few traces of their residence in the land of tin and copper ! Perhaps they were too busy working the mines, and shipping off the produce, to think of other matters? Anyhow, the fact remains that Cornwall is singularly poor in Roman relics. Here, at Fowey, for instance, we can only boast of one visible connecting link with our former masters, and that one only affords indirect proof of their presence hereabouts. This interesting relic, colloquially known as the " Longstone," lay, for many years, in a forlorn and neglected state, on the side of what is supposed to have been the Roman road between Fowey and Lostwithiel, about a mile from the former place. On one side of this long shaft of granite may be observed a rude attempt at letter cutting, but these mystic characters, which only provoke mirth on the part of the uncultured Briton, teem with meaning to the archæologist. In the first place, he assures you, with a confidence that begets conviction, that the inscription, in its perfect state, undoubtedly ran thus : " Hic jacet Cirusius Cuniwori filius," and then goes on to explain, that this granite shaft was put up, somewhere, to mark the spot where all that was mortal of a certain Cornish gentleman, and chieftain, of olden times was deposited, explaining, further, that when the Romans left Cornwall they handed over the care of it to one Karras, Esq., or Carausius, or, as his tombstone has it, plain Cirusius, who they seem to have regarded as their factor, or land-steward, for, on returning, somewhat unexpectedly, we presume, and finding this fine old Cornish gentleman ruling right royally on his own account—very much at home, in fact, after 18 years' possession, they tried to persuade him to render some account of his stewardship, failing which, and hearing that a polite invitation to become once more a Roman subject had been declined, these rude interlopers sent over one Alectus, who slew this Cornish worthy.

Truly fertile is the imagination of the Antiquary! It has even been asserted that this sturdy Home-ruler kept his ships near by, in the harbour of Polkerris, overlooking which he is said to have lived in his official residence, where fancy delights in picturing good old Karras disporting himself in the bosom of his family, with madame in the background superintending the preparation of Cornish cream!

With this brief and imperfect peep into the dim mists of the past we must perforce be content, for, at this point the curtain drops again, and we hear nothing more of this part of Cornwall till the Norman Conquest. We may be pretty sure that, with the departure of the Romans, Cornwall—like other remote parts of our Island—relapsed into pristine savagery, receiving few visitors, other than the sea-rovers, who flitted backwards and forwards from their Scandinavian strongholds, and founded settlements on the British sea-board.

⭺ Chapter II. ⁜⭠

In the Golden Days.

THE first real history of the parish of Fowey, Mr Rashleigh tells us, begins just before the Conquest.† Quaint old Leland, writing of these times, tells us that " the townlongged to one Cardinham, a man of great fame, and he gave it to Tywardreath Priory, but at this gift Foey was but a small fischar towne." This gift had more to do with the making of Fowey than might be supposed, for the monks of Tywardreath exchanged their produce with the Abbeys in Normandy, using Fowey as their place of shipment. By this means Fowey was opened up a second time to foreign trade, while foreigners came over and formed themselves into trading guilds. Very strange were the methods of Royalty in those days by way of encouraging trade : thus, when the King wanted ships he requisitioned those of Fowey, but, instead of paying for these services he allowed the owners to recoup themselves by the capture and plunder of any vessels that came in their way—a sort of legalised piracy. But the consequences of this free and easy way of squaring accounts were not wholly satisfactory, for, according to Mr. Rashleigh, "in a very short time the guilds got the upper hand of the Crown, and being foreign settlers the King found he had no control over them, and they became thorough sea-going pirates, and were as dangerous to his own ships as to his enemies." From this time forward piracy seems to have been the bane of the coast. Fowey—as indeed it deserved, suffering as much as other places, for, not only was its church destroyed by pirates,* but Tywardreath Priory, near Par Bay, was so roughly entreated by the sea-rovers that the monks begged leave to retire inland out of harm's way, shewing that fighting enemies of flesh and blood was not exactly in their line of business.

† See Note 1.
* See Note 2.

In spite of these drawbacks, Fowey now started off on a prosperous career, which was only brought to a sudden stop in later times by the indiscreet zeal of its inhabitants.

The way in which this "small fischar towne" suddenly blossomed forth into one of the chief naval ports of the Kingdom, and won, through the valour and enterprise of its seamen, the privileges of a Cinque port, is an interesting chapter of national history. In old Leland's words, "The glorie of Fowey rose by the warres in King Edward the First and the Third, and Henry the V. day, partely by feates of warre, partely by pyracie, and so waxing riche, fell al to marchandise, so that the town was haunted with shippes of diverse nations, and their shippes went to all nations." At this time the Fowey fleet is said to have numbered forty large ships, commanded by one Nicholas Kirriel. And it was with this fleet that the Foyens first won their spurs in naval warfare. "It was no small triumph to Fowey," says Mr. Rashleigh, "after Winchelsea had destroyed Portsmouth at Simon's request for the Duke Edward to come to Fowey, and be supported with their fleet of forty sail, when the total number of the Cinque port fleet was only fifty, and then, single-handed, to beat the enemy at Winchelsea. For this action, which saved the Crown, they were allowed to take away the Winchelsea chain, and become a Cinque Port in its stead." And thus was consummated the glory of Fowey. For the rest, hear what Carew says : " During the warlike reigns of our two valiant Edwards, the first and third, the Foyens addicted themselves to back their Prince's quarrel by coping with the enemy at sea, and made return of many prizes ; which purchases having advanced them to a good estate of wealth, the same was—when the quieter conditioned times gave means— heedfully and diligently employed, and bettered, by the more civil trade of merchandise ; and in both these vocations they so fortunately prospered, that it is reported sixty tall ships did at one time belong to the harbour ; and that they assisted the siege of Calais with forty-seven sail."

Gilbert, another writer, says that the Fowey contingent consisted of forty-seven ships and 770 mariners, while Plymouth on the same occasion only furnished twenty-six ships and 606 mariners, so that Fowey had every reason to be proud of her achievements. Nor were her efforts confined to the sea, for Fowey men assisted at the Battle of Crecy, of glorious memory, supplying, it is reported, the Duke's army with "many spirited and active young men, who did honour by their exploits to the country whence they sprung." Of the Fowey men who gained special distinction on this memorable occasion was one John Treffry, who, according to family documents, was made a knight banneret at Crecy, and had an honourable augmentation to his arms given to him for his signal services on that occasion.

The Commander of the Fleet at this time was Frissart Bagga, who, according to tradition, was buried in the Lady Chapel, and "whereof," says Carew, "there is some memory in the chancel window." All traces of this dashing sea captain have long disappeared from the church, and his name is only handed down on the authority of the old chroniclers.

How far our good Foyens proved themselves worthy of the high privileges attaching to their newly-won distinction remains to be shown. Of their courage and enterprise there can be no two opinions, but unfortunately the spirit of greed seems to have outrun their sense of duty and fealty to the Sovereign from whom their privileges had been derived. The sequel is thus felicitously described by Carew: "Hereon, a full purse begetting a stout stomack, our Foyens took heart at grass, and chancing about that time (I speak upon the credit of tradition) to sail near Rye and Winchelsea, they stiffly refused to veil their bonnets at the summons of these towns, which contempt—by the better enabled seafarers reckoned intolerable—caused the ripiers* to make out with might and main against them; howbeit, with a more hardy onset than happy issue, for the Foy men gave them so rough entertainment at their welcome, that they were glad to forsake patch, without bidding farewell; the merit of which exploit afterwards entitled them Gallants of Foy. Moreover, the prowess of one Nicholas—son to a widow, near Foy—is descanted upon in an old three-man's song, namely, how he fought bravely at sea with John

* See Note 3.

M. Shore

A LANE IN FOWEY.

Dorey—a Genoese, I conjecture, sent forth by John the French King, and, after much bloodshed on both sides, took and slew him in revenge of the great rapine and cruelty which he had committed upon the Englishman's goods and bodies."

The Gallants of Fowey were not, however, permitted to carry on their depredations, unchecked; for the French, stung to desperation by the piratical proceedings of the Fowey ships, which in spite of the truce continued to seize, burn, or destroy every foreign craft that came in their way, determined on giving the Fowey people a lesson they would be slow to forget, and sent the Lord Pomier with a fleet to destroy the town. This occurred in July, 1457, and is thus described by Carew:—"The Lord of Pomier, a Norman, encouraged by the civil wars, wherewith our realm was then distressed, furnished a navy from the River of Sayne, and with the same, in the night, burnt a part of Foy, and other houses confining; but upon the approach of the country's forces, raised the next day by the Sheriff, he made speed away to his ships, and with his ships to his home."

It was on this occasion that Place House was so gallantly defended by the wife of Sir Thomas Treffry during his absence at Court. Leland thus speaks of it:—"The Frenchmen diverse tymes assailed this town, and last most notably about Henry the VI. tyme, when the wife of Thomas Trewry the II., with her men, repelled the French out of her house in her housebande's absence." It was of course only right and proper that this valiant act should be commemorated as an ensample for future generations, and Leland tells us how "Thomas Trewry builded a right, fair, and stronge embateled tower in his house, and embateling all the vaultes of the house, in a manner made it a castelle, and unto this day it is the glorie of the town building in Foweye."*

The memory of this gallant exploit was still further perpetuated some sixty years ago, by the insertion of a stone figure of this same Elizabeth Treffry over an ancient gateway in the walls of Place, with an inscription underneath setting forth her achievements.

* See Note 4.

And now came a turn in the fortunes of Fowey, brought about
chiefly by the unscrupulous behaviour of its citizens, and, from
this check, the place never afterwards recovered. According to
Leland it came about in this wise :—" When warre in Edward the
IV. dayes, seasid bytwene the Frenchmen and Englisch, the men
of Fowey used to pray (spoil), kept their shippes and assailed the
Frenchmen in the sea agayn King Edwarde's commandment ;
whereupon the capitaines of the shippes of Fowey were taken and
sent to London and Dertemouth men commanded to fetch their
shippes away, at which time Dertemouth men toke them in Fowey,
and toke away, as it is said, the great chain that was made to be
drawn over to the haven from towre to towre."

Carew gives us a rather more detailed account of this
humiliating episode, thus :—" Our Foy gallants, unable to bear a
low sail in their fresh gale of fortune, began to skim the sea with
their often piracies (avowing themselves upon the Earl of Warwick,
whose ragged staff is yet to be seen pourtrayed in many places of
their church steeple, and in diverse private houses), as also to
violate their duty at land, by insolent disobedience to the
Prince's officers, cutting off (among other pranks) a pursuivant's
ears, whereat King Edward the IV. conceived such indignation as
he sent commissioners unto Lostwithiel (a town thereby), who,
under pretences of using their service in sea affairs, trained
thither the greatest number of the burgesses ; and no sooner
come than laid hold on, and in hold, their goods were confiscated,
one Harrington was executed, the chain of their haven removed
to Dartmouth, and their wonted jollity transformed into a sudden
misery : from which they strived a long time in vain to relieve
themselves ; but now, of late years, do more and more aspire to a
great amendment of their former defects, though not to an equal
height of their first abundance."

And thus ended the naval glory of Fowey.

The fortifications of Fowey in those old days were of a very
simple description. The earliest reference to them occurs in
Leland, who says that " In Edward the IV. day two stronge
towers were made a little beneth the town, one on eche side of
the haven, and a chayne to be drawen over." These two towers,

of which that on the eastern side is the only one still remaining in
its original form, are the sole existing monuments of the golden
age of Fowey. As regards the "chayne," no details have been
preserved concerning its dimensions, or of the way in which it
was worked ; but in the year 1776 a trawl boat fished up two
enormous links of iron which are said to have been a part of this
defence. These curious relics are preserved in a grotto, near the
beach, at Menabilly.

⇢✻Chapter III.✻⇠

In Troublous Times.

AND now we reach a period in the history of Fowey when its prosperity was in some measure revived through the energy and mercantile enterprise of the Rashleigh family who settled here during Henry VIII. reign. Says Carew:—" I may not pass in silence the commendable deserts of Master Rashleigh, the elder, descended from a younger brother of an ancient house in Devon, for his industrious judgment and adventuring in trade of merchandise first opened a light and way to the townsmen's new thriving and left his son large wealth and possessions, who (together with a daily bettering his estate) converteth the same to hospitality, and other actions fitting a gentleman well affected to his God, Prince, and country."

That the spirit of enterprise and love of adventure which had formerly so conspicuously distinguished the " Foyens " had not altogether died away during the long period of adversity through which they had passed, is clearly shown by the achievements of the " Frances of Fowey " at this period. Mr. Rashleigh says : " We cannot wonder at the Rashleighs being proud of the ' Frances of Fowey,' as their ship was called, for by its voyages the fortunes of the family were made. John Rashleigh, its master, went in most of the voyages of his cousins, Sir Francis Drake and Sir Walter Raleigh. Of the vessels that went with Frobisher to America ' The Frances ' was one. Of the little fleet that dared to face ' The Invincible ' the ' Frances of Fowey,' with Rashleigh her commander, together with his little pinnace ' Christopher,' steered by Capt. Moon, were two. Their services then, in England's hour of danger, were thought worthy of being rewarded by the nation with £500; moreover, the amount of bags of Spanish gold which the family letters shew had been seized from the Spanish galleons testify to the gallant work performed by this small craft

An Old Manor House.

REMAINS OF AN OLD HOUSE ON BULL HILL.

of 140 tons, manned with 70 townsmen from Fowey. The vessel was afterwards captured, when with Drake on his last voyage, and its loss caused, it was said, the death of that great Commander. For nine years it remained in the hands of Eustace the archpirate, but was freed at last by Capt. Whetburne, of Dartmouth, and returned to its owner, and afterwards went several voyages with Drake's successors."

The memory of this gallant little vessel has been preserved in the name of the "Ship Hotel," whose quaint front still looks down on passers-by in much the same way as it did 200 years ago. The way in which this house of call for travellers—but formerly the abode of the Rashleigh family—came to be entitled the "Ship" is thus explained by Hals:—"In remembrance and memory of this ship, they caused the figure of it to be perpetuated in a small ship, about five feet long, made and formed by a ship carpenter, of timber, with masts, sails, ropes, guns, and anchors, and figures of men thereon, which is hanged up to the roof, or planking, with a iron chain in their old house in this towne, of which ship those gentlemen have often given me ocular observation as well as told me the above history of the premises in the time of Charles II." Of this most interesting model no traces whatever remain beyond the name, the family having migrated, many years since, to their beautiful country seat of Menabilly, a mile or two West of Fowey.

Though greatly altered since those days, so as to bring its interior economy more into harmony with modern requirements, one room at least in the "Ship" remains much as it was when the abode of the Rashleighs, with its ornamental ceiling, fine oak panelled walls, and carved chimney piece with the date of its erection 1570, "by John Rashleigh and Alse his wife," son of the famous Philip*.

Fowey never again recovered its ancient position of naval importance. Apart from the humiliations which had been put upon it, other causes were at work to keep it in a secondary position as a port, namely, the growing importance of Plymouth

* See Note 5.

and Falmouth, where greater facilities were offered for the accommodation of large fleets.

During the first half of the 17th Century, and especially during the civil wars between King Charles and his Parliament, the history of Fowey is closely bound up with that of the Kingdom at large, and for this reason full of interest. The town was occupied for some time by the Parliamentary troops under the Earl of Essex, and it was at this time that, in consequence of the Royalist tendencies of its inhabitants, it suffered much damage. The Rashleigh house, especially, seems to have been marked out as a fit and proper object for the destructive soldiery to wreak their vengeance or by way of showing their abhorrence for the opinions of its owner. Mr. E. Rashleigh tells us that it was " sacked by Essex's troops when they visited Fowey in Sept. 1644, upon which occasion they destroyed £1,000 worth of property in it, which act made Jonathan Rashleigh declare in after years that he had only the bare walls left."

This Jonathan Rashleigh was Chief Commissioner to the Mint for this part of Cornwall, and being well-known as a zealous supporter of Charles I., suffered imprisonment in St. Mawe's Castle at the hands of Essex, who, with his officers, made himself very much at home in the Manor House at Menabilly during the enforced absence of its master. Marks of this occupation are still visible on the wainscoted walls of the dining room, in the shape of sword cuts on a panel where hung a portrait of King Charles, the sight of which moved the Parliamentary officers to such a pitch of indignation that they drew their swords and hacked the portrait to pieces.

A great deal of the family plate was cut up into money at Menabilly House in aid of the Royal cause ; it is said also that some heavy ordnance, which defended the old house in the town of Fowey, was presented to the King at the same time—a welcome addition, doubtless, to his somewhat scanty equipment of war material.

It was close to Fowey that King Charles, when on a reconnoitring expedition on the hill overlooking the town, had a narrow escape of being shot by a rebel sharpshooter. A cotemporary writer gives the following account of this episode, of which he was an eye witness :—" Saturday, 17th August, 1644, His Majestie attended with his owne Troop, Queen's Troope, commanded by Captain Brett, and sixty commanded troopers went to Cliffe, from thence his Majestie went to Lanteglos, to the Manor House, belonging to the Lord Mohun, just over against Foye, where his Royall person ventred to goe into a walk there which is within halfe musket shott from Foye, where a poore fisherman was killed in looking over at the same time his Majestie was in the walke, and in the place where the King a little afore passed by."

Think how nearly the whole course of English history was changed by this little bullet—shot, possibly, at a venture !

The "poore fisherman" was not the only innocent sufferer for the mistakes of his betters !

The walk "where his Royall person ventred to goe" on this occasion is one of which the Foyens of modern times are justly proud, for, besides its great antiquity, the views from thence of the harbour and coast on a bright day are such as can hardly be matched for beauty and variety in any part of Cornwall. Carew, who wrote in 1602, gives the following description of the Hall Walk: —" Amongst other commodities, it (Lord Mohun's Manor House of Hall) is appurtananced with a walk, which, if I could as plainly shew you, as myself have oftentimes delightingly seen it, you might and would avow the same to be a place of diversified pleasings : I will therefore do my best to trace you a shadow thereof, by which you shall (in part) give a guess at the substance. It is cut out in the side of a steep hill, whose foot the salt water washeth, evenly levelled, to serve for bowling, floored with sand for soaking up the rain, closed with two shorn hedges, and banked with sweet scenting flowers, it wideneth to a sufficient breadth for the march of five or six in front, and extendeth to not much less than half a London mile ; neither doth it lead wearisomely forth right, but yieldeth varied, and yet not over busy turnings, as the ground's opportunity affordeth ; which advantage increaseth the prospect, and is converted on the foreside into platforms for the planting of ordnance and the walkers sitting; and on the back part into summer-houses for their more private retreat and recreation. In passing along, your eyes shall be called away from guiding your feet, to descry, by their farthest kenning, the vast ocean, sparkled with ships, that continually this way trade forth and back to most quarters of the world. Nearer home they take view of all sized cocks, barges, and fisherboats hovering on the coast. Again, contracting your sight to a narrower scope, it lighteth on the fair and commodious haven, where the tide daily presenteth his double service of flowing and ebbing, to carry and re-carry whatsoever the inhabitants shall be pleased to charge him withal, and his creeks·(like a young wanton lover) fold about the land with many embracing arms. The walk is guarded upon the one side by Portruan, on the other by Bodyneck, two fishing villages; behind, the rising hill beareth off the cold northern blasts; before, the town of Foy subjecteth his whole length and breadth to your overlooking, and directly under you, ride the home and foreign shipping; both of these in so near a distance, that without troubling the passes or borrowing stentor's voices, you may from thence, not only call to, but confer with any in the said town or shipping."

There is a charming little romance associated with this walk and the Manor of Hall to which it belongs. It is related that in 1330, a young lady, Elizabeth by name, only daughter and heir to Sir John Fitzwilliam, the Lord and Master of Hall, was dwelling quietly at the Manor House, when some gay young soldiers of sporting proclivities were driven into Fowey Harbour, through stress of weather. As was natural with young fellows thus situated, they lost no time in following their favourite pursuit, with results to one of the party, which were little foreseen. Let us follow Tonkin's account of this little *affaire de cœur*. "They say that Sir Reginald de Mohun coming into the harbour with a company of soldiers bound for Ireland, and landing, let fly a hawk at some game which killed it in the garden of Hall, when Sir Reginald Mohun going for his hawk, and being a very handsome personable young gentleman, qualities which his descendants retained to the last, the young lady fell in love with him, and having a great

AN OLD INN, BEFORE RESTORATION.

fortune, the match was soon made up between them by consent of their friends on both sides." Let us hope that Sir Reginald never regretted the good fortune which brought him into Fowey harbour and enabled him to kill two birds with one stone."

This Manor of Hall remained in the possession of the Lords Mohun up to the time of the Revolution, when it passed into the hands of Governor Pitt. Tonkin, who wrote in 1733, says :— "There is now but little left of the old house, which I believe was destroyed in the Civil Wars, and might incline the Lord Mohun to part with it." The old house has long disappeared, its site is occupied by a comparatively modern farm house ; but the Chapel, which stands a short way off, still exists, though in a sadly dilapidated condition, being used as a barn and implement store. There is a handsome doorway, tolerably perfect, while the waggon roof of good English oak still remains intact and as sound as the day it was put up. A raised walk, with a south aspect, behind the present house, marks the site of the old garden ; and here, fancy delights in picturing young and handsome Sir Reginald courting his "faire ladye" on this same plaisaunce, under the shade of spreading sycamores, or in the arbour which once adorned the end of this terrace-walk. The old bowling green may still be traced in the middle of an apple orchard.

Can we wonder, then, at the Foyens of modern times liking to shew their friends the "diversified pleasings" of the Hall Walk, with all its old time associations of love and war ?

➤✳ Chapter IV. ✳◄

The Decline.

FOWEY had scarcely recovered from the effects of its occupation by the Parliamentary forces when it was attacked by a very different sort of foe—to wit, the Dutch Fleet, under De Ruyter. The way in which this came about, and how the Fowey gallants beat off the enemy's ships, is it not all written in the old Chronicles? The story will bear repeating, for it is probably known only to a few, and is notable, chiefly, as the last occasion on which the Foyens saw a shot fired in anger. It was a gallant fight too, and for that reason worthy of being held in remembrance. To quote from Hals—" At the mought of this harbour are two petty bulwarks, most famous for a fight they had with a Dutch man-of-war of seventy guns, doubly manned, that was sent from their main fleet of eighty sail that cruised before this haven, 16 July, 1666, then in pursuit of our Virginia fleet of eighty sail, which, escaping their cognisance, safely got some hours before them into this harbour, and on notice given of the war, sailed up the branches thereof as far as they could, and grounded themselves on the mud lands thereof. Nothwithstanding this, the Dutch vessel resolved to force the two forts aforesaid, and to take or burn our said Virginia fleet. Accordingly it happened on that day, a pretty gale of wind blowing, this ship entered the haven, and as soon as she came within cannon shot of those forts, fired her guns upon the two blockhouses with great rage and violence, and these made them a quick return of the like compliment or salutation. In fine, the fight continued for about two hours time, in which were spent some thousands of cannon shot on both side, to the great hurt of the Dutch ship, in plank, rigging, sails, and men, chiefly because the wind slacked, or turned so adverse, that she could not pass quick enough between the forts, so as to escape their bullets, but lay a long time a mark for them to shoot at, till she had opportunity of wind to tack round, turn back and bear off at sea to their fleet, to give them an account of her unsuccessful attempt and great damage as aforesaid, to the no small credit and reputation of Foy's little castles, manned out with gunners and seamen from the ships of the Virginia fleet for that purpose, who all, by reason of the walls and entrenchments thereof, were preserved from death, notwithstanding the continual firing of the cannons of the Dutch men-of-war upon them, whereby the contiguous lands by the bullets were ploughed up, to the terror and astonishment of all beholders. After this engagement, the cargo of the whole Virginia fleet was landed at Foy, and gave opportunity to the townsmen to buy much tobacco at a very cheap rate, which instantly upon the conclusion of the peace between England, France, and Holland, was sold in this kingdom, France and Spain and Holland at a dear rate, and much enriched the townsmen thereby, as Mr. Major, one of the merchants, informed me." So that, after all, the Foyens had no reason to regret the putting in of "our Virginia fleet." "'Tis an ill wind that blows nobody any good!"

Gilbert gives a somewhat different version of this famous fight, and the discrepancy in the dates rather leads one to infer that there must have been two attacks on "Foy's little castles." After telling us that "On the 20th May, 1667, a bold but unsuccessful attempt at invasion. was made by the Dutch fleet, under Admiral De Ruyter, which was frustrated by the bravery of the Devonians and Cornishmen," he goes on to relate how, "notwithstanding all these polite proceedings and fair promises" on the part of De Ruyter, after he left Plymouth Sound, two of his men-of-war anchored off the Harbour of Fowey and endeavoured to destroy the works newly raised at the entrance, but after continuing a fire from their great guns for an hour and a half, they were compelled to retire with their sides battered in by the heavy shot from the shore, the loss of one of their masts, and several men killed and wounded, without any injury to the Cornish. After this they were seen to hover about the coast, but without making any further attempts on Devon or Cornwall.

The castle which bore the chief brunt of this attack is the one still standing on St. Catherine's Point, built in Henry VIII.'s reign. As evidence of the ardour of the attack, it may be mentioned that up to within recent times shot of different sizes have been found amongst the rocks under the castle, besides being ploughed up in the fields at the back. Old men relate how, when boys, they remember piles of shot, which had been turned up by the plough, laying about in ditches, and around the farm buildings. Some of these have been brought together and placed in the vestry of Fowey Church for their better preservation. One can picture the excitement in old " Foye towne " while this great fight was in progress, and the rejoicings that took place when the inhabitants saw the Dutchmen turning their broad sterns to the forts, after receiving the punishment they had courted.

The fight with the Dutchmen was the last occasion on which the Foyens were afforded an opportunity of " making history." Since then, for some 200 odd years, the town may be said to have had no history worthy of being recorded. We may conclude, therefore, that her " Gallants " settled down to quiet, plodding ways, minding their own affairs, and leaving others to pursue their several vocations in peace and quietness. The wars with France, during the last, and the early part of the present century, afforded opportunities for the young bloods to emulate the deeds of their fathers, and to prove themselves worthy scions of the men who beat the " rippiers" of Rye and Winchelsea ; but of their achievements, alas ! there is no certain record—public spirit seems to have fled the place, and the " light of other days" to have gone out. Nevertheless, such brief entries as the following, in the Annual Register, give us an inkling of what was going on, in the " dark ages," of Fowey :—" Letters from Fowey state the arrival there of the Lord Middleton, richly laden with cocoa, indigo, coffee, quicksilver, valued at £45,000, taken by the Maria, privateer, of this port." And again : " Came in the Earl St. Vincent, 14 guns, Captain Richards, privateer, of this port, with the New Harmony of Altona, from Smyrna to Amsterdam, with cargo valued at £80,000." And so on, to the end of the chapter. It is known too that the Fowey and Polruan ship-builders turned out several smart privateers. There is also a story handed down in a local family about an ancestor who took part in an engagement off the harbour mouth, when a Fowey cutter attacked a French privateer, and rammed her with such good effect that she sunk, while those of the crew that escaped drowning were sent as prisoners of war to Plymouth.

Nor were our good Foyens in any ways backward in the prosecution of the illicit trade ; but that is another story ! Suffice it to say here, that, if the local records are tantalisingly silent on this particular subject, official documents are sufficiently explicit to enable us to gather some idea of the activity and enterprise with which this particular industry was carried on, up to within the last fifty years. Here, for instance, is one extract from contemporary accounts, which may be taken as a sample :— "Came in the Eagle, excise cutter, Captain Ward, with a fine smuggling cutter called the Swift (formerly the Buonaparte French privateer), with 500 tubs of brandy, after a long chase within the limits of the Dodman."

But, if the Fowey folk of modern times have abandoned the more than questionable practices by which the "glory" of their town was formerly established, they have never lost their predilection for the sea. Young Fowey, male and female, takes to the water as naturally as young ducks ; every lad seems to regard the sea as his natural heritage, and follows a seafaring life as a matter of course. Thus it comes about that everyone in Fowey is in some way connected with shipping, and the arrival and departure of the most insignificant coaster is of more vital interest to a considerable section of the populace than the fall of a Ministry. No stranger can be long in Fowey, indeed, without becoming alive to the aquatic proclivities of the people. Whether in the train, rattling along between Par and Fowey, waiting at the station, or strolling through the " circumbendibus " streets, the one fact, which beyond all others forces itself into notice, is the intimate connection between the people and the sea. By the sea, they may be said, in very truth, to live and move and have their being. And this is rendered all the more noticeable by the universality of the title " Captain," or plain " Cap'n," as Fowey folk call it ; indeed, the word so often greets the ear here, that, in a spirit of mischief, the stranger might be tempted to speak of our good Foyens as consisting of some 1,500 souls, mostly Cap'ns! That such a large proportion of the male populace should have risen to this position of honour and profit is very much to their credit, and certainly speaks volumes for the industry and enterprise of the present generation.

The nautical tendencies of the people crop out sometimes in queer and unexpected ways. Thus, at public entertainments, concerts, and the sundry mild forms of dissipation, which, before the demon of progress broke loose in the town, were congenial to the soul of the Foyen, the audience were wont to mark their approval by loud shouts of "An-chor," "An-chor." There was a nice homely ring in it, though whether the greeting had a deeper meaning than is at first apparent, the philologist must decide. Simple folk might interpret it into an invitation to cast anchor — in other words, to throw in their lot with the good Foyens! The idea is a pleasant one, at any rate; but this and many other agreeable traits of the people are fleeing before the besom of progress, and soon a Foyen will be hardly distinguishable from the average Briton of other parts.

To be thoroughly convinced, for once and for all, of the entire harmony existing between the Foyens and their sur-roundings, the natives must be seen *chez luis*—on regatta day, for instance (Lerryn regatta day, for choice)—when everything capable of conveying a human being on the surface of the water, in tolerable safety, is called into requisition, and all Fowey sets off on the first of the flood to join the throng that will shortly assemble in one of the sweetest little spots in fair England. Young men and maidens, old men and boys, all lend a hand, and you may see now how deftly a Fowey girl can handle an oar, losing little, if anything, by a comparison in this respect with the sterner sex.

An hour or two afloat, during the summer months, is, in fact, quite part and parcel of the every day life of the Fowey people; and, no doubt, it is this fondness for the oar that accounts for the fine development of the Fowey maidens. One can only express the sincere hope that this healthy taste may always be cultivated and encouraged; and, in this respect, one cannot but be struck with the advantages which the young women of our coast towns, such as Fowey, possess in their ports and rivers, with their opportunities of healthful recreation as compared with their less fortunate sisters of the inland towns. And when, to the accomplishment of rowing be added a good voice and a love of song, it requires no great stretch of imagination to picture the charm of a moonlight trip on a warm summer's eve, in pleasant company. If music hath charms to soothe, the charm is infinitely enhanced when it comes rippling across calm water on a still night, and especially when accompanied by the human voice. Such an experience is by no means uncommon in Fowey Harbour, and the recollection of it lingers pleasantly in the memory for long after.

Then, again, picture a calm, sunny morning in the haven. The ships, with their sails loosed to dry, all steeped in warm sunlight; the mists, lingering over Pont Pill, or being drawn up by the sun's rays from off Polruan, like a veil; the wake of a boat cuts across the dark water with a line of molten silver, each splash of the oar striking like a glint of fire, and a fishing-boat, with its red-brown sail all aglow with colour, drops with the last of the ebb past the old castle and disappears round St. Catherine's Point; while from one of the ships comes the cheery singing of the crew, as they shorten in cable and prepare for a start. These anchor-songs, or "chanties," with their rattling chorus, have a most exhilarating effect, especially if sung with feeling and spirit, and this effect is greatly heightened when, as in Fowey Harbour, the opposite hills echo back the voices.

The mention of echoes recalls to mind a humorous episode of days gone by. One calm summer's night at Fowey, long after all respectable folk had retired to roost, the quiet of the harbour was suddenly broken in upon by a voice from the landing, hailing a vessel in mid stream "Mary Jane, ahoy!" but as no response came back, the hail was repeated. Still no reply from the Mary Jane. The hail was repeated, again and again, and in the crescendo scale, with the same lack of result. Not a breath rippled the glass-like surface of the water, and the night being singularly still the shout came back, thrice repeated, each time, by the echo, with all the distinctness of the original. The effect was ludicrous in the extreme : it seemed, indeed, as if some Polruan wag across the water was chaffing the poor fellow left thus forlorn on the landing. Like the owls on Winander's shore, the echoes would shout :—

> " Across the watery vale, and shout again,
> Responsive to his calls,—with quivering peals,
> And long halloos, and screams, and echoes loud
> Redoubled and redoubled : concourse wild
> Of mirth and jocund din ! "

For one long hour did the poor fellow continue his appeals to his faithless Mary Jane, with varying intonation, from a moan of despair to shrieks of frenzied rage that were absolutely comical. And no Mary Jane condescended to answer after all !

So far, we have noticed only the pleasing aspects of the aquatic proclivities of the people. There is a dark side to the medal. Who shall speak of the agonies of mind suffered by wives, sisters, and mothers, when the equinoctial gales are shrieking through the streets of Fowey, and storm-tossed craft are running in to seek the friendly shelter of the haven? Anxious eyes are straining through the driving scud to catch a sight of the well-known vessel, and hearts are wracked with anguish, of which the world wots not : for " reported missing " is an old, old, and ever renewed story in this little Cornish haven, and few there be here who have not tasted of the bitterness which these words bring to the loving heart which has nothing left for it now but to bide patiently the time when the sea shall give up its dead, and fond hearts shall be joined once more.

THE PANELLED ROOM, SHIP HOTEL.

➜✳ Chapter V. ✳←

Recent Times.

CURIOUS feature of Fowey, and closely connected with the habits of the populace, is the "water-port," with which almost every house on the harbour face is provided, and which bespeaks the amphibious character of their owners. A great part of Fowey has, in fact, been built on ground, stolen, as it were, from the harbour, and, raised even now, but a little way above ordinary high-water mark : thus, it comes to pass that once, or perhaps twice every year, the strange spectacle is presented of Market Square and a great part of Fore Street converted, for the nonce, into a lake, when the sea, in a spirit of playfulness, foreign to its accustomed mood, meanders in and out of shops and private dwellings, to the detriment of cellars and underground stores.

The water-ports are sometimes turned to curious uses. Thus, at the top of Fore Street stands an interesting relic of former days, in the shape of a mansion which can be traced back for at least a couple of hundred years. It has a beautiful porch, the delight of artists, is clothed in creepers, and has three windows looking askance at you from a roof fairly bowed down with its weight of years. In the dining room, with its panelled walls, there once stood a handsome mantlepiece,—and thereby hangs a tale. The absence of this ornamental appendage is thus accounted for :—A former tenant, a Frenchman, finding, after a brief sojourn there, that business engagements, of a pressing nature, required his presence elsewhere, vanished from the scene, took French leave, it is presumed, accompanied by the mantle-piece shipped off, so it is said, through the "water-port." The Frenchman and the mantlepiece were never afterwards heard of !

The street alignment of Fowey, if, indeed, the term "align-ment" can be applied to the hole-and-corner arrangement of the place, is suggestive of a time when wheeled vehicles were unknown, and pack-horses were the principal " conveyancers." Hence, the navigation of the chief thoroughfares taxes, not only the patience and skill of drivers, but the agility of pedestrians, who must, perforce, make a bolt into doorways or passages, to avoid annihilation, when anything of the nature of a " trap " is sighted ; from which it may be gathered that pavements, or side-paths, would be useless and inconvenient excrescences, at the present time. Very suggestive, too, of the old-world character of the place is the fact that before the advent of the bustling little railway, from Par, the main thoroughfare of the town was blocked at each end, to anything bigger than a donkey-cart, by a kind of archway or transverse room, over the street, a relic, it is said, of a time when a watchman held office here, and took stock, and toll, of everything that passed in, or out. May not this provision have also afforded convenient " bolt-holes " for gentlemen who were " wanted " in connection with the particular branch of trade which, in former days, engrossed so much of their time and attention, hereabouts?

The advent of the railway was the signal for an outburst of local enterprise that proved fatal to many an interesting link with the past, and presently took shape in the erection of a real Hotel " first-class," replete, too, with every modern convenience. But the climax of this spirit of unrest and innovation, let loose by the railway invasion, was the Hotel Bus, which must needs rattle backwards and forwards to the station, in a noisy, self-assertive way that threatened to carry desolation and mourning into many a Fowey home. And thus, was the death-knell sounded of another link with the past, for, to make way for the intrusive Bus, the arch-ways at each end of the street, quaint memorials of byegone days, were taken down, and every trace of their existence removed.

But it would require a chapter, or two, to render adequate justice to the alterations and " improvements " that Fowey has witnessed during the last thirty or forty years, and by which many interesting associations have been swept ruthlessly aside and the susceptibilities of all true lovers of the picturesque wantonly offended. The old King of Prussia, for instance, immortalised by Mrs. Parr in her romance of Adam and Eve and once a favourite subject for artists, has been smartened up beyond recognition, and many another house has shared the same fate.

The reader may possibly wonder what benefits the King of Prussia conferred on the Fowey folk, that they should have bestowed his title on an Inn. The King of Prussia, thus immortalised, may possibly have been a certain noted smuggler of Mounts Bay, William Carter, by name, who there built himself a stronghold and defied the King's cutters for a time. Prussia cove was where he hailed from, and he was ever after known by the title of the King of Prussia. This, I say, is a possible explanation of the name, and if the correct one furnishes another link with a forgotten past.

Local customs and peculiarities are rapidly disappearing before the progressive broom which was introduced with the railway, but there is one "religious observance" which dies hard owing to the hold it has obtained on the rising generation of Foyens :—the May Day celebration, to wit. The ceremonial observed on this occasion, may thus be described. During the few weeks immediately preceding the festive day, young Fowey industriously and surreptitiously collects all the old tin pots from the dust heaps, and other sources well-known to the experienced in these matters. These are secreted out of reach of the local guardian of the peace, whose devotional instincts are not to be implicitly trusted, and, on the eve of the 1st, are brought together and deftly tied to each other, forming a huge bunch of sound-emitting instruments. When light begins to dawn in the eastern sky, young Fowey emerges from its respective lairs, assembles around the tin trophy, and then, all "tailing on," they drag it in triumph through the principal streets of the town, to an accompaniment of shouts and yells. If the representative of law and order has not broken in on the procession, the tinkling cymbal is dragged to the outskirts of the town, where the "religious rites" are consummated,—supposing the needful sinews of war to be forthcoming, by the purchase of Cornish Cream, which is eaten under the shelter of a hedge. "This," says our local antiquary, "is nothing more than a relic of the worship of

Apollo, as carried on even now, in Andrieux, in the province of Hautes Alpes, France."

It was the remark of a profound observer of human nature, that the religious belief of a people, however corrupt or degraded, should never be destroyed without putting something better into its place. This excellent precept is but little heeded by the rude innovators of the nineteenth century, and there is reason to fear that when the May-Day celebration is finally suppressed there will be nothing left, of equal attraction, in the opinion of its devotees, to take its place.

Another old belief, which has fled before the demon aforesaid, was in the superlative attractions of "Par Stack," and Luxullyan Viaduct. In the "good old days," for a visitor to these parts not to have heard of those local "gigantic gooseberries," was to argue himself unknown, and to fall many degrees in the estimation of the town's folk. "When I first came to these parts," said a friend speaking of old Fowey days, "I had to admit, as many had done before me, the deficiencies of my early education, and I at once prepared, in a becoming spirit of humility, to remedy this defect, by making acquaintance with these vast monuments of provincial enterprise; I went, I saw, but I cannot honestly say I admired. The step from the sublime, in fancy, to the commonplace in reality was indeed a brief one."

Let it here be recorded, for the benefit of the inexperienced, that the Par Stack is only a tall chimney attached to a smelting works, while the mighty Luxullyan Viaduct, which an ecstatic compiler of a "Handbook to Cornwall" refers to, as "thrown across the valley with astonishing audacity," is nothing but an ordinary viaduct, as viaducts go now-a-days.

Of the varied charms of this little haven and river, with its ramifying creeks and "pills," it is difficult for an admirer to speak without seeming exaggeration. What pen, indeed, can adequately paint the ever-changing beauties of their wooded banks, or touch in their varying tints, in spring and autumn, or describe the unique charms of the St. Winnow shore, or the "voluptuous loveliness" of the Saw-mill creek, the romantic attractions of Pont Pill, or the weird associations of Penpool. On one side, Gollant smiles on

OLD HOUSE IN FORE STREET.

you from a setting of fruit blossom ; while, on the other, Cliffe peeps out of its daffodil beds, where it has slept peacefully on these three hundred years past; and, further on, Lerryn hides its sylvan charms up a tidal creek, as if shunning the too pressing importunities of its admirers, where the trees along the water's edge bathe their feet and dip their arms in the intermittent stream, and nature seems all repose.

And then, twice in the twenty-four hours, the salt water runs back again to old ocean, as if, in very shame at its rude intrusion into scenes of such peaceful and pastoral beauty, leaving great ugly scars of mud and rock, out of sheer wantonness, or, perhaps, by way of reminding us of the important part that water plays in the scheme of nature's landscape compositions. But there, the sea was always a fickle friend, and a vengeful foe, with as many moods as an April day !

Nor is this fair tract of country,—apart from its unique historical associations, lacking in interests to satisfy the most diversified and exacting tastes, — artistic, aquatic, or merely nomadic. The man would, indeed, be hard to please who failed to discover any source of pleasure in the manifold attractions of this most fascinating of neighbourhoods, where sea, river, and land blend into one harmonious whole, and where a luxuriant vegetation will be found toying with the Atlantic waves ; while a tangle of sea-water creeks wander far inland, amidst green pastures, shady woods, and blossoming orchards, till lost finally amongst the pebbles of some purling brook.

But to see Fowey at its best, you must choose a fine day in early spring, when the gardens are overflowing with the delicate white Alyssum—"Snow on the Mountain," as it is most appropriately styled here in Fowey—and the walls, and even roofs, are one blazing glory of pink Valerien—" Pride of Fowey," as they call this most sociable of British weeds. Away out, towards the harbour mouth, the cliffs are purple with the wild hyacinth, flecked here and there with masses of the white ox-eyed daisy ; while down by the water's edge, the storm-beaten rocks seem to have been converted for the nonce into the loveliest of spring gardens, every nook and corner glowing rose colour with the delicate

Thrift, or sea-pink, contrasted by the white of the bell-shaped
Bladder Campion and the grey-green Samphire.   The air, too, is
laden with the peach-like scent of gorse, wafted across the valley
from that cloth of gold spread on the hill side yonder to the west.
The sea, too, has a translucence all its own here, and if its pea-
cock hues of green and blue are not so startlingly vivid as on the
north shore, the extent, and variety of view, and the graceful
contour of the coast line, make ample amends for any deficiencies
in this respect.   Certainly Fowey has its charms, and little as the
quaintness and quiet of the place may commend it to the
" Cockney tourist and intrusive prig," with his notions of " life "
and " smartness," there are few spots in the West Countrie where
a more enjoyable holiday can be spent, or that offer so many
attractions to the artist, the antiquary, or the archæologist—to say
nothing of the fisherman and the boating man.

(NOTE.—It may be as well to state that since the foregoing was
written many old and familiar features of the place have been
"improved" beyond recognition.   Consequently, those who knew
Fowey in its quieter and more homely days, and now revisit it,
will be tempted to exclaim, in the words of the poet :—

" It is not now as it hath been of yore ;
Turn wheresoe'er I may,
By night or day,
The things which I have seen I now can see no more !")

NOTE 1.—See "A Short History of the Town and Borough of Fowey," by E. W. Rashleigh, Esq.

NOTE 2.—For an account of this most ancient and interesting edifice, see "St. Fimbarrus Church : Its Founders and their History," by Henry M. Drake, M.A.

NOTE 3.—The old English word for basket was "rip," hence the men who were employed in hawking the fish about came to be called "rippiers." ("Ancient Rye"—a lecture by Rev. A. T. Saville.)

NOTE 4.—*Fowey*.—The derivation of this word seems to be wrapped in a good deal of mystery. Halse says—"The name Fowy is a contraction of Foys-wye, *i.e.*, Walls Holy River. Fois is derived from Foys-Fenton, Walled Well, or Spring, near Alternunne, the fountain from whence the river Fowye fetcheth its original. . ." Tonkin says—"That the town of Fowey took its name from the river, I make no doubt of. Leland calls it in Cornish, Fowathe ; Carew and Camden, Foath ; which may probably signify, upon the river Fowey, as composed of Fowy-arth." In an old Customs book, of 1713, the name is spelt Fowye ; while, in a book of earlier date (1681), we find it written "ffowy." To come to recent times, if the name was rendered phonetically, it would be spelt Foy ; though, curiously enough, when asking for a ticket at Paddington, it is necessary to pronounce the word as it is now spelt.

NOTE 5.—During the "restoration" of the Ship Inn, in 1891, a curious relic, in the shape of a large swing signboard, was discovered in an attic, where it had probably lain for 100 years or more. One side of it showed an English sloop engaged with a French frigate, while on the other was depicted a full-rigged East Indiaman. The paintings were evidently the work of a good artist, and it is thought they may have been done by Opie, at a time when he lived about in public-houses, and squared accounts by painting signboards. This interesting relic having come into the possession of W. Gundry, Esq., of Torfrey, he placed it in the hands of a good artist for restoration, and had the board split in half, so that the two pictures might be framed and hung. They each measure about 5½ft. by 4½ft.

"All ages of a nation are leaves of the self-same book."—*Renan.*

—

PART II.

—

A

WAR DIARIST OF THE 17TH CENTURY.

BEING AN ACCOUNT OF

King Charles' personally conducted Campaign in Cornwall,

WITH MANY CURIOUS AND INTERESTING PARTICULARS OF

The Fighting around Lostwithiel and Fowey,

AND

The Surrender of Essex's Army at Castledore.

CONTENTS.

ERRATA.

Page 32, line 7, for *narative* read *narrative*.

LOOKING OVER LANTIC BAY.

H. Shore

A WAR DIARIST OF THE 17th CENTURY.

→⚜ Chapter I. ⚜←

Introductory.

IT would be interesting to know how many, if any, of the tourists who flock into " far Cornwall," year after year, ever give a passing thought to the historical associations of the scenes through which they pass. Not a large number, probably, and yet, it was here, on the very neck of the promontory formed by the Fowey river and Par Bay, with the old-world town of Fowey at the apex, there was enacted one of the most tragic episodes in the grim drama of the Great Civil War. It was on the very ground that the line passes over between Lostwithiel and Par, that King Charles won his last victory over the Parliamentary forces, before the tide turned finally, and overwhelmingly against him, the closing scene, the surrender of Essex's army, taking place on the high ground to the southward. Two hundred and fifty years, with all their changes, have rolled by since that September day, in the year 1644, and yet the story has lost none of its pathos. It is one, indeed, that, from the very magnitude of the interests involved, must ever appeal forcibly to all who have English blood in their veins, nay, must possess a profound interest to every member of the great English-speaking race. For the quarrel between Charles and the Parliament about the Ship Money, and other matters, was fraught with consequences to the Western World which the combatants little foresaw, and from whatever standpoint we view the fratricidal struggle a pathetic interest attaches to the particular phase of it with which this corner of England is associated, that the most prosaic mind can hardly be indifferent to. Even now, after the lapse of centuries, one occasionally chances on individuals, sane enough in ordinary matters of business, who, at the mere mention of the quarrel lose all mental balance, and wax fiercely eloquent about the perfidy of the King, or the encroachments of the Parliament, according to the side they champion. This is a fine spirit, of course, even, if one cannot altogether share the feelings of such fiery disputants, and though it is difficult even now to read the story of the war without being carried away, and wishing success to one side or the other, it ought, nevertheless, to be possible to discuss the matter dispassionately, and with due regard to the fact, that, neither side enjoyed a monopoly of virtue.

The most common attitude of mind towards the past, however, is one of sheer indifference, from which it is difficult to rouse people. Perhaps this is due to deficiencies of early education. It may be that if the School Histories from which we gathered our youthful ideas of the past had been compiled in the lively and graphic style of the modern "war correspondent," we should have taken a deeper interest in our studies, and have looked on the scenes of great historical events with livelier feelings. It certainly does seem as if the compilers of School Histories sometimes went out of their way to invent a special language for the purpose of disguising their meaning. Armies never have a good square fight: they " meet," or " encounter," or " engage," and then " retire after suffering severe losses," though what they lose is not always explained—it may be their money, or their clothes? What, for instance, does the sentence, " the war was now prosecuted with great vigour," convey to the intelligence of the average school-boy? His thoughts revert to the board he saw stuck up in a wood, the last time he went nutting, " trespassers will be prosecuted with the utmost rigour of the law." Or again, to say that " in the West of England, where King Charles conducted his army in person, the campaign proved more favourable to him," conveys little idea of fighting ; it is more suggestive to the youthful mind of the King leading his soldiers by the hand, or of some elderly verger "conducting a party" round a cathedral! The most enthusiastic admirer of this department of literature can hardly maintain that school history-books are exactly redolent of cannon smoke, or of garments rolled in blood, and, until the compilers condescend to use the language of every-day-life, our British youth can hardly be expected to take a deep interest in the struggles of their fore-fathers, or even to read the " romances called history," without experiencing a feeling of boredom.

And, even supposing the desire to conjure up the past is really latent in the mind, one's endeavours are too often hampered by the changes which time and the hand of man have wrought on the face of nature. Happily, however, there are still a few corners of the land which have escaped from the devastating effects of man's " civilizing mission," where the lover of the past and the student of nature may wander undisturbed through sweet meadows, and by the side of murmuring brooks, without having his pleasant dreams broken in upon by the prosaic "hullo there!" of the owner of a cabbage-plot, or infuriated proprietor of a suburban villa. Such a locality is that around Fowey and Lostwithiel, where nature's fair garb has perhaps suffered less mutilation from the causes above-named than most inhabited portions of our island. Here the pedestrian may wander as he listeth, over hill and dale, following the promptings of his own sweet will, and study a corner of England rendered classic, for all time, by reason of its associa-tion with one of the most stirring periods of our history. And, certainly few excursions are likely to prove more thoroughly enjoy-able or profitable than a quiet ramble over the scenes whereon were fought out the closing episodes in King Charles' "personally conducted" campaign in "far Cornwall." So little has the country changed, while so graphic is the account that has been preserved, that one may follow the movements of the Royal and Parliamentary troops over every foot of the ground, from the moment when Essex, in the words of the historian Green, "by a fatal mistake plunged into Cornwall, where the country was hostile," till the shattered remnant of his army surrendered as prisoners of war, to the King, at Castle Dore.

For a singularly interesting narrative of the campaign we are indebted to an officer of the Royal army, Richard Symonds by name, an Essex gentleman, who kept a diary of events, from day to day. The entries herein are so ample and precise that we may trust to them as implicitly as to a modern guide book ; and that the compiler was not only an observant officer, but a gentleman of culture is evident from his narrative. He had, moreover, a taste for topography and genealogy, and this taste, notwithstanding the arduous duties of his calling, he found the means of gratifying. With this officer for our guide there will be no difficulty in following the incidents of the war, hereabouts ; while for a vivid and realistic picture of the times it would be difficult to match the simple, straightforward narrative of this Royalist officer.

A few explanatory remarks touching the positions of the contending forces at the time the story begins, will make things clear to the reader. Be it understood, then, that the Parliamentary forces under the Earl of Essex having committed the primary error of "plunging into Cornwall," where the populace was hostile to the cause, they found it necessary to retreat on Lostwithiel, to be near their new base of supplies at Par, closely followed by the Royalists, under the personal command of the King, who on August 2, 1644, took up his quarters at Boconnoc, Lord Mohun's seat, about five miles to the eastward of "Lestithiel," as it was then called, the foot being drawn into the enclosures between Boconnoc and the heath, "all the fences to the grounds of that county," as the historian Clarendon justly observes, "being very good breastworks against the enemy," the horse being mostly quartered between Liskeard and the coast. In this position the armies lay within sight of each other for three or four days : Essex in hopes of a relieving force coming up in the rear of the King, while Charles, acting on the advice of a council of war, had decided to await the arrival of Sir Richard Grenville, with reinforcements of foot and horse, before attacking the rebels.

This piece of "masterly inactivity" on the King's part had unfortunate results, for "that inconvenient spirit that had possessed so many of the Horse officers," appeared again. It seems that these malcontents had been persuaded by certain "officers of quality," who had been taken prisoners from Essex's army, that their Chief was only kept from coming to terms through fear that "when the King had got him into his hands, he would take revenge upon him." And so, these "Politick Contrivers," thinking that an arrangement might be come to, and further fighting prevented, concocted a letter to Essex, and actually prevailed on the King, contrary to his convictions, he being fully persuaded in his own mind that it would have no better result than his own letter to the rebels, sent a few days before, to allow it to be despatched. One does'nt need to read very carefully between the lines, here, to see that the discipline of the Royal army was not altogether such as a well-regulated army ought to have displayed : but of that anon. Next day came my Lord Essex's reply, " My Lords, in the beginning of your letter you express by what authority you send it. I, having no authority from the Parliament who have employed me, to treat, cannot give way to it without breach of trust. My Lords, I am your humble servant, Essex." Brief and to the point, there was nothing left now but to fight it out !

Meanwhile, Sir Richard Grenville advancing from Truro took possession of Lanhydrock, Lord Robartes' seat, a few miles north of Lostwithiel, as well as Resprin Bridge, thus opening up communication with the King's army.

On the 13th the Royalists still further improved their position by the seizure of the pass of St. Veep and the ford across the river Fowey at Cliffe, as well as View Hall, belonging to Lord Mohun " over against Foy," where was a small fort (Pernon), on a point near by, commanding the town and harbour of Fowey, " both which places were found so tenable " says Clarendon, that " Capt. Page was put into one, and Capt. Garraway into the other with two hundred commanded men, and two or three pieces of ordnance, which these two Captains made good and defended so well, that they made Foy utterly useless to Essex, save for the quartering his men ; nor suffering any provisions to be brought into him from the sea that way." Essex's oversight in allowing these important positions to be seized by the Royalists without a struggle cost him the greater part of his army. " It was exceedingly wondered at by all men," says Clarendon, " that he being so long possessed of Foy, did not put strong guards into those places."

By these operations the rebels were effectually boxed up in the Foy peninsula, their only possible bolt-hole being commanded by the Royalist guns.

➳✠ Chapter II. ✠⬰

The Rebels are Driven into Lostwithiel.

" NOW the King had leisure to sit still, and warily to expect what invention or stratagem the Earl would make use of." Just as Wellington sat still, in after times, and watched Massena from the lines of Torres Vedras.

Essex deemed a waiting game to be his best chance, while Charles, conscious that he had got his opponent into a trap, was willing to allow matters to drift on. In this situation the two armies lay facing each other for eight or ten days without any occurrence of note taking place. And at this juncture of affairs let us take up the thread of Richard Symonds' narrative :— " Satterday, 17 August, His Majestie, attended with his owne troope, Queen's troope, commanded by Capt. Brett, and sixty commanded troopers went to Cliffe, in S. Veep, where Colonel Lloyd, the Quartermaster General's regiment lyes to keep the passe. The enemy keepes the passe on the other side at the parish of Glant (S. Sampson's). From thence his Majestie went to Lanteglos to the Manor House belonging to the Lord Mohun, just over against Foye, where his Royall person ventred to goe into a walke there which is within halfe musket shott from Foye," and where the circumstances already narrated took place. " A little below are some of our great pieces that command the towne of Foye, and beyond that a fort of ours that commands the entrance into the mouth of Foye haven, in the parish of Lanteglos. This house, walke, &c., being gotten by the vigilant care of Sir Jacob Astley, Major Generall of his Majestie's army, three or four days before. At night his Majestie, &c., returned to their quarters."

We can easily picture the sensation which the sight of the Royal cavalcade, plunging through the narrow lanes that intersected this part of the county, would cause amongst the quiet country folk, and how their loyalty would be stirred to its depths. The little hamlet of St. Veep, with its quaint old church still stands, as peacefully, and almost as far removed from the world's bustle as it did on this August day of the year 1664 with the "passe of Cliffe" below, but little altered in its outward aspect.

The Lord Mohun's Manor House "over against Foye" has disappeared, but the "walke, within halfe muskett shot of Foye," may be visited and the view admired under pleasanter circumstances than were vouchsafed to his Majestie. The visitor may even identify the spot where stood "our great pieces that commanded the towne of Foye," while at the end of the walk, on a promontory jutting out into the harbour, some traces may even be detected of the "fort of ours that commanded the entrance into Foye haven." At the same time it is easy to understand how a few guns on the Foye side of the river might make the walke unpleasantly hot for those who "ventred" in.

As to the "fort of ours," commanding Foye haven, it proved a veritable thorn in the side of the Parliamentary Generals, who, when too late, discovered their mistake in not previously seizing the position. In a Parliamentary "diurnal" of the time, we read that "The enemy daily encroacheth upon our quarters, the loss of Fowey harbour being to our infinite disadvantage, no ship being able to ride out of the command of their guns. The Lord High Admiral made a gallant attempt on Monday, 26th of August, to have cleared that side of the enemy, whereby his ships might harbour as at first, but extremity of weather would not suffer him to land any men, so that he is now returned safe into the sound."

To continue the diary :—

"Sunday, 10 August.—Some of the rebell horse came within the Lord Mohun's Parke, but their boldnes was presently forced to fly.

"Tuesday.—Proclamation that all stragling foot presently repair to their colonels, upon payne of death."

The commisariat of those days was in its infancy, and if the soldiers would keep their bellies stocked they had to forage around on their own account.

This proclamation was owing to the King's determination to bring matters to a head at once, as reports had reached him of a

M. Shore.

THE FERRY LANDING, AS IT WAS.

Parliamentary relieving force, marching westward. He therefore decided, in Clarendon's words, "either to force Essex to fight or to be uneasy, even in his quarters."

"Wednesday, 21 August.—The King's troope and Queen's troope marched in the night from Liskeard to the leaguers at Boconnock. About five in the morning, being very misty, the King's army and Prince Maurice's was drawn out (Clarendon tells us that the army "under Prince Maurice was looked upon as distinct, and always so quartered"), and about seven they marched on to the top of the high hill* that looks into Listithiel. The body of foot and cannon lay all this day on this and the adjoining hill, being on each side flanked with horse and a reserve of horse, consisting of the Earl of Cleveland's Brigade behind the foot. A commanded party of 1,000 foot, led by Coll ——, of Prince Maurice's army, gott on a hill this side of the river neare the towne, where at bottom was a passe. The small cottages which were on this hill next the towne were all this forenoon a burning. Our foot and their's pelting one at another all day; small harme done to our's. The enemy shott a great many pieces of cannon at them, and at the left wing of our horse, little or no hurt. Thus stood both armyes all this day on this side. But Sir Richard Grenville, with 700 men, on the other side, pelted the rogues from their hedges between the Lord Roberts, his house, and Listithiel, and near Trinity (Restormel) Castle (in Lanlivery), which castle was this morning surprised by Sir Richard Grenville's men, and some thirty of the rebells taken, and divers barrels of beefe. This day Major Smythe, that commanded a party of horse neare this castle, who did most gallantly, was shott with a musket bullet; yet living. At night, Sir Richard Grenville's men retired. Towards night the body of the King's foot gott into the close on the hills of the left and right side of the playne that goes down to Listithiel, and in the night planted many pieces of our cannon. That hill on the left hand neere the Chappel of St. Neeton's in the parish of St. Twynoe (St. Winnow) was commanded by a party of about 1,000, led by Colonel Apleyard. The hill opposite was kept by Prince Maurice his army."

* See Note 1.

Evidently there was a mutual disinclination to come to close quarters. The chiefs being well aware of the indifferent materials of which their respective armies were composed, would hesitate at risking all on the issue of a pitched battle.

"Thursday, Aug. 22.—This day we mainteyned in all parts what we had gott in the night, many of the enemy's great shott of 9lbs. being shot at our men. One of our cannon shott luckily hit a party of the enemy's horse, and killed two horse, and one horse leg shott off at once. Most part of this day the King's and Queen's troope faced the enemy on the top of the playne doing duty. This night upon the top of the highest hill and in the middle between our hedges and the enemyes hedges our men made a work twenty yards square, notwithstanding the enemyes shott.

"Friday, 23.—The work on the top of the hill aforesaid next the said chappel seemed in the misty morning to the enemy to be a body of horse, as some of their centryes were heard to say. They shott a piece of 9lb. many times at this worke, killed one and hurt another, that was all the hurt was done to us this day at the work. On Sir Richard Grenville's side Colonel Champernown of Devon, colonel to the Prince Maurice, leading up his foote neere Trinity Castle, was shott in the neck: his own men tooke off his sword and cloake and left his body, which the enemy took. Since by a drummer, we hear that his wound is not mortall. This half of the day fine, four in the morning till twelve. The King's troope and Queen's, with Prince Maurice, faced on the plaine the day before. All the afternoon a commanded party of both troopes wayted on the King there till night. Then we returned to our quarters in the field as the two nights before; mornings and evenings being very mysty; through the night starlight.

"Satterday, 24 August.—Being the day of St. Bartholomew, the forenoon was spent in great shot from them to our battery. No harme; we got many of their bullets. About xii. of the clock, his Majestie went down to court to dinner; his troope and the Queen's troope drew off them too, having been there ever since the day began. In the afternoon, about three of the clock, the King went upon the hill, and divers came and told him the enemy was gone towards Foye, for indeed none, or very few of them, could be seene; about two of their cannon played some time, and some muskets. Almost all that were there, besides the King and Prince Maurice, were of opinion they were gone.

"Sunday, 25 August.—His Majestie went into the field upon the hill at three in the morning attended as before, the morning being very wett and windy; presently sends word to the Prince his army to know if they were marching, and to tell them he was here and ready, and that he conceived it a fit morning to doe the business, likewise he sent the like to Sir Jacob Astley to tell his owne army so. Preparations on all parts of the King's side; his horse are come into the field, half of them gone over to Sir Richard Grenville's side. An hourly expectacion of our readiness to fall on: Prince Maurice about twelve of the clock comes armed, and tells the King he was ready, and asked the King if he were so: ymediately their resolution altered, and our troopes were sent to Liskard. Long before this 'twas evident enough that the enemy was not only hid from the danger of our battery, but was *toute preparé* to receive us. 'Twas appointed for the Westerne army to fall on first."

→✣ Chapter III. ✣←

Sir W. Balfour and the Cavalry break out.

MONDAY.—This day 2,000 horse and 1,000 foot of the King's went to Westward behind the enemy to stopp the landing of provisions by sea, and to hinder their foraging Westward by land. Also this day came to us 100 barrels of powder, &c., from Pendennis Castle and much from Dartmouth.

The question of supplies was, at this particular time, a pressing one, as will be seen from the following letter, written by a distinguished Royalist :—

Lostwithiel, Saturday, Sunset, 1644.

Deare Wiffe,—This messenger will tell you how affayres goe here and in these lande parties. Here is infinite want of match. For God's sake send to Mr. Lone as soon as this comes to yr. hands, and cause him with all speede to press horses and bring away six hundredweight of match from the Mount to this army, first to Lostwithiel and thence to the army, which I hope in Jesus Christ will so bless us as we shall be free and merry and joyfull again in Cornwall. . . My Lord Mohun has lent me £100. I trust my friend Rolle will doe at least the like ffriendship, and I am sure you will procure what possibly you can, if it be but six-pence. My love is just and full to you still. Pray let Jacke write to me truly what match he has in all ; and I conjure you both to get as much as possible to be made with all possible haste, and at what cost so ever. Send to Fubbs for all his oakum. I write in as much haste as ever in my life. I love you and Jane, and John, and Bess. God give me good news of you all and of poore Punch.

Dear hart, love still your own harty part.—F. BASSETT.

I thank Christ I am very gracious with King and Prince—I hope wh. all. To Mrs. Bassett, my deare wiffe, at her Tehidy.

It may not be out of place at this particular juncture, while

the Royal army is foraging for "match" and powder, to make the
reader acquainted with the artillery for which the items in question
were needed.

As far as one can gather, a gun was something in the nature
of a "white elephant" that required to be treated gingerly, if it
was to last through a campaign; it had a knack of getting hot and
bursting; "One may fire ten shots an hour if the pieces be well-
fortified and strong ; but if they be but ordinary pieces, then eight
is enough ;" so say some regulations of the Civil War days. What
would have been thought of a Maxim gun ? Not even
Cromwell and his ironsides would have faced that ! To continue,
" After forty shots you must refresh and cool the piece, and let her
rest an hour, for fear lest eighty shots should break the piece, not
being able to endure the force and heat." How far off all this
sounds now ! As regards the position of artillery in action, the
guns were usually posted between battalions of infantry, as was
the case at Naseby. If possible, an eminence was chosen,
" because the shot come with a deal more power down hill than
up hill ; and as one shot from a hill-side may go through two or
three ranks when that which is shot upward cannot pass through
one." It was sometimes objected to this that the shot were liable
to roll out of the muzzle, to which another writer retorts that in
such a case "they are simple men that charge (load) them."

A gun's crew consisted of but three men—the gunner, his
mate, and "an odd man, to serve them both, and help them
charge, discharge, mount, wad, cleanse, scour, and cool the piece
being overheated," besides covering up the powder barrel after
loading, to prevent an explosion. There was even a system of
drill, approved doubtless by the Commander-in-Chief, consisting
of thirteen words of command, commencing with the very
necessary caution that a gunner should go to work "artist-like" to
charge his piece, carefully avoiding the spilling of powder, "for it
is a thing uncomely in a gunner to trample powder under his feet,"
and winding up with this solemn appeal to his vanity and self-
respect :—" Let the gunner endeavour to set forth himself with as
comely a posture and grace as he can possibly ; for the agility and
comely carriage of a man in handling his ladle and sponge and

loading his piece, is such an outward-action as doth give great
content to the standers-by." It was fitting that the nursery maids'
feelings should be considered in the exhortation !

The movement to the Westward, "behind the enemy" above
mentioned, was fraught with disastrous consequences to Essex—
the loss of St. Blazey and Par, where his supplies were landed.
The Parliament's forces were now completely hemmed in on the
promontory, and Essex, finding himself in a " tight place," began
to devise means of escape. Sir Wm. Balfour was directed to try
and break through the King's lines with the cavalry, while Essex
purposed embarking, together with the foot, at Fowey. But, unfortunately for the success of these plans, Fowey Harbour was
commanded by the Royalist guns. The sequel will be made
clear by the diary :—

"Saturday, Aug. 31.—The night before the King had notice
(being at Boconnock, his troops at Laureath) that the enemy was
marching away. General notice was given thereof at one of the
clock in the night. His troop and the Queen's came to Boconnock,
whither came news that the enemyes horse were then upon the
downe, and coming up betweene the hills where our whole army's
leaguer was, but most of our foote were straggling 3 parts by 4."

To enable the reader to understand what had taken place, a
few words of explanation may be necessary. It will be remembered
that the pass on the East side of the Fowey river at Cliffe was in
the hands of the Royalists, while " the enemye kept the passe on
the other side at Glant," or Golant, as the village is now called.
The importance of these positions will be evident when it is stated
that they commanded the lowest point at which the river was
fordable, and therefore the only spot where it was now possible
for the Parliamentary cavalry to break out.

On Aug. 31, according to Clarendon, two foot soldiers, one
of whom was a Frenchman, deserted to the Royalists, and assured
the King "that it was intended that night, to break through with
their horse, which were then all drawn up on that side of the river,
and town of Listithiel ; and that the foot were to march to Foy,
where they should be embarked." This intelligence agreeing with
what had already been received at headquarters, orders were at

once issued, " That both armies (the King's and Prince Maurice's). should stand to their arms all that night; and if the horse attempted an escape, fall on them from both quarters."

The width of the river here, as Clarendon truly says, is "but a musket shot over," and on the Royalist side was commanded by a small cottage well fortified and garrisoned by fifty musketeers; while orders had been given, and were now renewed, to break down the bridges, and cut down the trees near the highway to obstruct the passage of the horse.

For the rest, we cannot do better than follow Clarendon's account of the affair :—" The effect of all this Providence was not such as was reasonably to be expected. The night grew dark and misty as the enemy could wish, and about three in the morning the whole body of the horse passed with great silence between the armies, and within pistol-shot of the cottage, without so much as one musquet discharged at them. At the break of day, the horse . were discovered marching over the heath, beyond the reach of the Foot, and there was only at hand the Earl of Cleveland's Brigade, the body of the King's being at a greater distance. That brigade, to which some other troops which had taken the alarm joyn'd, followed them in the rear, and killed some, and took more prisoners. But stronger parties of the enemy frequently turning upon them, and the whole body often making a stand, they were often compelled to retire ; yet followed in that manner, that they killed and took about a hundred."

The King's feelings—and language on hearing of the enemy's escape must be left to the imagination of the reader. It was certainly enough to make a saint sware, let alone a Stuart, and the misfortune cost Charles dearly in his subsequent campaigns. Who was to blame ? Symonds being a gentleman and a soldier, leaves the role of criticising his superiors, while on active service, to others. Clarendon, who wrote long after and was hampered by no such prejudices, is explicit enough. Here is his version of this shameful episode : " The notice and orders came to Goring," who. be it observed, commanded the King's Horse " when he was in one of his jovial exercises ; which he received with mirth, and slighting those who sent them, as men who took alarms too warmly ; and he continued his delights, till all the enemy's Horse were passed through his quarters, nor did he pursue them in any time." Thus was Sir Wm. Balfour enabled to lead his 2,000 Horse right through the King's lines, and clear away into Devonshire by way of Caradon, Pillaton, and Saltash, and " even to London, with less loss or trouble than can be imagined, to the infinite reproach of the King's Army, and of all his garrisons on the way."

A Sovereign could scarcely have been worse served, and with such a broken reed as Goring to trust on, small wonder that the unhappy monarch fared so badly later on *vis-a-vis* with the stern soldiers that Cromwell brought up to oppose him. The curious thing is that no one was shot, or even brought to trial, for this grave dereliction of duty :—" Nor was any man called in question for this supine neglect," says Clarendon, " it being thought not fit to make severe inquisition into the behaviour of the rest, when it was so notoriously known how the superior officer had failed in his duty."

A LANE IN GOLANT.

Chapter IV.

The Retreat on Castledore.

DIRECTLY the retreat of the enemy's Horse became known Symonds tells us that " The Earl of Cleveland, with those of his brigade, viz. : most of his colours, but not above one hundred of 400 men, faced the enemy on the hill, but did not, nay dare not, charge them, as Lieut.-Colonel Leake told us : when the King came up we saw most of their body of Horse, on the hill near Bradock upon that downe, ymediately the Earle of Cleveland's Brigade and the Queene's regiment followed them and charged their rear. The King, supposing they would go through Liskeard and Launceston, sent two messengers of our troop, Mr. Brooke and Mr. Samuel West, with a letter to Sir F. Dorington (who hath 1,000 horse in Devon) to stop their march. But the enemy went not near Liskeard this day, but went right to Saltash to ferry their horse over into Devonshire. In this interim his Majesty lost no time, but with those foot he had (which God knows were very few, most of them being stragled abroad the country for provision) and with his owne troope and the Queen's, marched towards Listithiel. On the hill next beyond the towne were bodyes of the enemyes foot with colours left in their reare to make good their retreate ; their baggage, artillery, and the rest of Essex his foot army having marched all the night towards Foye. At 7 in the morning the King's forlorne hope of foot consisting of about 1,000, entered Listithiel without much opposition, their foot still retreating.* And after that his Majestie had commanded two or three pieces of cannon to be placed in the enemye's leaguer, to command the hill where their foot reserve stood. the enemye's reserve marched away, our forlorne following them in chase from field to field in a great pace. About 8 of the clock his Majestie with the two troops passt over the river on the south side of

* See Note 2.

Listithiel, where the enemy had left a cart load of muskets, besides many more in the durt, a little higher five pieces of cannon in several places, two of them being very long ones.   With this small force his Majestie chased them two myles, beating them from hedge to hedge.   Being come neare that narrow neck of ground betweene Trewardreth Bay and St. Veep Pass, the rebels made a more forcible resistance ; then about 11 of the clock Captain Brett led up the Queen's troope and most gallantly, in view of the King, charged their foot and beat them from the hedge, killing many of them, notwithstanding their musquets made abundance of shott at his men ; he received a shott in the left arm in the first field, and one of his men, La Plume, a Frenchman killed ; yet most gallantly went on and brought his men off ; his cornett's horse shot with two other horses and two more wounded ; he retreated to be dressed, and the King called him and took his sword, which was drawn in his hand, and knighted Sir Edward Brett on his horse's back.

" This was just 12 of the clock.

" About this time we tooke seven or eight prisoners, whereof one was a Captayne of foot who was taken by Captain Brett's men, and another took one of their cannoniers, who was pitifully drunke, having shott off his cannon but once.   Now the King's foot came in apace and increased much.   Shooting continued much on both sides, more on theirs, we still gayning ground. About 4 of the clock some of the rebell's horse (they having two or three troopes with them) charged our foote, but the Lord Bernard ymediately got leave of the King to draw up his troope, who were all ready, and drew up to the rogues, standing their musket shott a long time ; but because their horse retreated and their foot lay so close under the hedges,* which are all cannon proof and have no avenues wider than one, or in some places two horse can approach at a time, and likewise because his Majestie sent to draw us off, wee fairly retreated ; one of the Queen's troope here was killed.   More of our foot coming up to relieve the rest.   By this time Colonel Goring, General of his Majestie's

* See Note 3.

horse, came to the King, having not heard of the enemye's march
till 10 of the clock. Now was our foote in great bodyes gote upon
the high hill, just in the narrowest passage of land between
Trewardreth Parish Church and the passage over the river which
runs by Listithiel. Just at 6 of the clock the enemy made a very
bold charge, both of cannon, muskets, and horse to gain this hill,
as likewise the passe near St. Veepe, but were valliantly beaten off,
and our men not only keeping both but gott some ground also;
this heate lasted about an houre; at first it was so hott that the
Lord Bernard drew out his Majestie's troope with the colours (for
the time before we left them with the King) to charge the rebells,
but General Goring mett us and told him the room was too little
for horse and our troopers to charge too, and advised he would
please to face a little and draw off to the King. Here was of the
Queen's troope one shott in the sholder. With our troope was
drawn up the Queene's, Prince Maurice his lifeguard, commanded
by Arundel, and the Lord Hopton's, which was commanded by
Sir Thomas Wilford of Kent; these made a brave body of about
200, all well armed.

"The King sending for us to come to him, and the enemye's
vollyes abating and ceasing, wee were drawn in the next close but
one where his Majestie was. And this was the chiefe of the
business of this day. Now did many of the enemye's cannon give
fire at our men till darke night. I saw a fellow of ours, drest as a
musketeer, who was shot in the chin, the sholder, and the hand,
by cannon at one shott.

"This night the King lay under the hedge, with his servants,
in one field. The troopes of Life Guards lay in the next, it being
very wyndy and crosse wind for Essex shipping of his men, and
rayned much and great stormes. I saw eight or nine of the
enemye's men dead under the hedges this day. Some shooting
continued all night. (Clarendon says the King's quarters were " so
near the enemy that they discharged many cannon-shot, which fell
within few yards of him when he was at supper)."

"Sunday, Primo Septembris.—This morning our army was in
the same place it lay in the night, and small or no shooting on
either side.

"The four Life Guards, about 7 of the clock, were sent to quarters ; we to Lanreth ; for all the pasture in those fields was eate up very bare by the enemyes horse, whome we had, in this time of stay, almost starved.

This morning, about 7 of the clock, Generale Goring was sent with the horse to pursue the enemye's horse, who, as the King was informed, were gotten into Saltash. Sir Edward Welgrave, de com. Norfolk, colonel of horse, tooke above one hundred of the rebells' horse in the pursuit on Satterday, and told the King that if the country had brought in intelligence but an houre or two sooner, where and which way they went, he believed they might have cut off and taken all their horse, they were such cowards and so fearful that eight (said he) would make twenty cry for quarter. Essex, his life guard commanded by Colonel Edward Doyley, went away with the horse, as wee heard. He, himself, was with the foot. This Sunday the rebells, being within but a little compass of ground (being surrounded by sea on three-parts, and our army on the land), and because their rebell generals, the Earle of Essex, Robert Devereux, and their Field Marshall, the Lord Roberts, with many others of their chiefe Commanders, had left, and went by sea, as they supposed, or they knew not which way. Skippon, now left in chiefe, being Major Generall, sent propositions of treaty to his sacred Majestie, who, out of his abundant mercie, notwithstanding having them all in so great advantage, was pleased to give them leave to march away with these condicions :—

"Leaving all their cannon, which were in all 42, and one morter. All their musquetts and pikes. All their carriages, except one to a regiment. To march away with their colours, and foot officers with their swords. Those officers of horse, with swords, hat bands, and pistolls.

"A waggon full of musquet arrowes, 100 barrels of powder. Munday, 2nd Septembris, 1644.

" His Majestie's army of foot stood on the same ground, or thereabouts, as before ; the several regiments by themselves, and the colours stuck in the ground flying.

" His Majestie in the field, accompanied with all his gallant cavaliers, dispersed in several places, while, about 10 of the clock,

Major Skippon, first, or in the front, marched with all that rout of rebells after the colours of their several regiments. These regiments I took a note of, after three or four had passed :—

Colonel Lord Roberts.

Colonel Bartlett.

Colonel Aldridge, blew colours, with lions, rampant, or,

Colonel Davies, white colours, citty of London.

. Colonel Conyngham, greene colours.

Colonel Whichcote, greene, citty London.

Colonel Weare, A, Govenor of Lyme.

Colonel Carr, Polius Karr xj, ensigns, or distinctions B.

These are Plymouth men ; they had more foot.

Colonel Layton, a regiment of horse B. Cornets.

All their ensigns and cornets were wound up veloped.

" It rained extremely as the varlets marched away a great part of the time. The King himself ridd about the field, and gave strict commands to his chiefe officers to see that none of the enemye were plundered, and that all his soldjiers should repair to their colours, which were in the adjoining closes. Yet, notwithstanding our officers with their swords drawne did perpetually beate off our foot, many of them lost their hatts, &c.

" Yet most of them escaped this danger till they came to Listithiel, and there the people, inhabitants and country people, plundered some of their officers and all, notwithstanding a sufficient party of horse was appointed by his Majestie to be their convoy.

" They all, except here and there an officer (and seriously I saw not above three or four that looked like a gentleman), were strucken with such a dismal feare that as soon as their colour of the regiment was past (for every ensign had a horse, and rid on him, and was so suffered) the rout of soldiers of that regiment prest all of a heape like sheep, though not so innocent : so durty and so dejected as was rare to see. None of them, except some few of the officers, that did looke any of us in the face. Our foot would flout at them, and bid them remember Reading, Greenland Howse (where others that did not condicion with them tooke them away all prisoners) and many other places, and then would pull their swords, &c., away, for all our officers still slasht at them. The rebells told us, as they pas't, that our officers and gentlemen carried themselves honourably, but they were hard dealt withal by the common soldiers.

"This was a happy day for his Majestie and his whole army, that without loss of much blood, this great army of rascalls that soe triumphed and vaunted over the poore inhabitants of Cornwall as if they had been invincible, and as if the King had not bin able to follow them, that 'tis conceived very few will gett safe to London, for the country people whome they have in all the march so much plundered and rob'd that they will have their penny-worths out of them."

Chapter V.

Surrender of Essex's Army to the King.

THIS "great army of rascalls," as our Royalist friend styles them, had not to wait long for their revenge. The following month, October 27, 1644, at Newbury, Charles found himself once more *vis-a-vis* of the Parliamentary army, which, we read, "was strengthened by the soldiers who had surrendered in Cornwall, and who wiped away the shame of this defeat by throwing themselves on the cannon they had lost and bringing them back in triumph to their lines," or, as another writer puts it, "they rushed at them with a will to give them the Cornish hug, as they expressed it, and rejoiced mightily over their recovery."

Several versions of this surrender of the rebel army and the negociations that led up to it have come down to us, all of which, while agreeing in the main, furnish details distinct from each other. One thing is certain, that no sooner had Essex sent an officer to the King to desire a parley, than, without waiting a reply, he set off for Fowey, from whence, accompanied by Lord Robartes "and such other officers as he had most kindness for," he took ship and escaped to Plymouth, leaving directions for Skippon to make the best terms he could for the army. In other words he left his troops on the lurch, to get out of the mess the best way they could. For the following particulars we are indebted to Whitelock's "Memorials of the English Affairs":—

"Skippon called together his field officers to a council of war, and, being more of a soldier than an orator, spoke plainly to them to this purpose—'Gentlemen, you see our general and many of our chief officers have thought fit to leave us, and our horse are gone away. We are left alone upon our defence. That which I propound to you is this, that we, having the same courage as our horse had and the same God to assist us, may make the same trial of our fortunes and endeavour to make our way through our enemies as they have done, and account it better to dye with honour and faithfulness than to live dishonourable."

In these same "Memorials" we get another glimpse of Skippon in the character of a soldier rather than of an orator. When the "city bands" marched out of London, two years before, Whitelock tells us that "Major-General Skippon made short and encouraging speeches to his soldiers, which were to this purpose : —' Come, my boys, my brave boys, let us pray heartily and fight heartily. I will run the same fortunes and hazards with you. Remember the cause is for God, and for the defence of yourselves, your wives, and your children. Come, my honest, brave boys, pray heartily and fight heartily, and God will bless us.' Thus he went on all along with the soldiers, talking to them, sometimes to one company and sometimes to another, and the soldiers seemed to be more taken with it than with a sett formal oration."

In a Parliamentary " diurnal " of the period, entitled " Perfect Occurrences," dated Sept. 6—13, and which, being an " Opposition paper," had of course to explain away the disaster, we are told that before the capitulation the army was attacked by the Royalist forces ; that General Skippon fought like a lion and animated his men to make such a brave resistance that the King was forced to yield to his proposals for a capitulation, and that amongst the details agreed on was a proviso that no soldier was to be moved to turn to the King except such as should come voluntarily.

Clarendon says that one hundred men did actually come over to the King's side. We also gather from him that the terms first proposed by General Skippon were " such as upon delivery of a strong fortified town after a handsome defence are usually granted, but they quickly found they were not looked upon as men in that condition." The terms really granted were—the officers to have liberty to wear their swords, and to pass with their own money, and "proper goods," and to secure them from plunder, they were to have a convoy to Poole or Southampton ; that all their sick and wounded might lay in Foy till they were recovered, and then have passes to Plymouth.

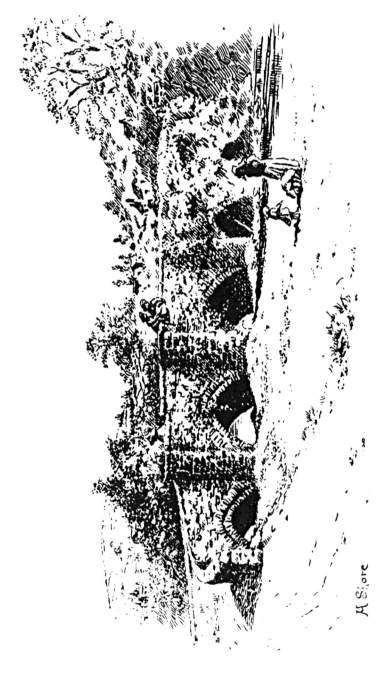

LOSTWITHIEL BRIDGE.

The force which surrendered to the King amounted to about six thousand men. It is not improbable that the strength of the position they held, and from which they could not have been driven without stiff fighting, may have had something to do with the favourable terms accorded them. Symonds says " They had a stronghold, and an hill, where was an old double-trenched fort wherein they had planted many of their great pieces. It would have been difficult to have beate them out of it : and then Foye was fortified."

This "double trenched fort" was the old British camp of Castle Dore, occupying a fine position on the narrowest and loftiest point of the Fowey promontory,—about equi-distant from Fowey and Lostwithiel, and commanding both sides, almost to the water's edge. The camp is a conspicuous object at the present day and is well worth a visit, if only to enjoy the magnificent panorama of St. Austell Bay and the country on all sides. Tradition even points to the farm of Lawhibet (pronounced "Le Whibbit"), on the eastern slope, as the scene of the negociations. Relics of those stirring times, in the shape of cannon-balls and bullets, are still occasionally turned up by the plough, while the scene itself, in its present unchanged aspect and perfect solitude, seems haunted by a thousand memories. Even now, as you survey it, in undisturbed quiet, you may picture to yourself, by the aid of such details as have been preserved, the closing scene in the stern drama that was enacted here, on that September morning in the year 1644.

The Royalist reader will be glad to hear that the " poore inhabitants of Cornwall," who suffered much at the hands of Essex's men in the course of their march through the county, did " have their penny-worths out of this great army of rascalls," on their return journey. It was late in the day before the terms of the surrender were settled, nevertheless, Clarendon tells us that " they would march away that night, and although all care was taken to preserve them from violence, yet first at Listithiel, where they had been long quartered, and in other towns through which they had formerly passed, the inhabitants, especially the women, who pretended to see their own cloathes and goods about them,

which they had been plundered of, treated them very rudely, even
to stripping of some of the soldiers, and more of their wives, who
before had behaved themselves with great insolence on the march."
So the British soldier had actually commenced travelling *en famille*,
at this early period! One can quite understand how the town
ladies would lord it over the poor provincials! On the whole,
then, we ma ytake it that the "rout of rebells," and their wives, had
a rough time of it, and one can understand, also, how, of all who
started, only about a third part ever reached Southampton, where
their convoy left them : upon which, says Clarendon, "Skippon
gave a large testimony under his hand, that they had carried
themselves with great civility towards them, and fully complied
with their obligation." In short the escort behaved as brave
soldiers and cavaliers should do to a beaten foe. Could it have
been of this detachment that a Parliamentary trooper wrote, when
he described a party of Royalist horse, in the following sarcastic
terms?—"First came half a dozen of carbines in their leathern
coats and starved, weather-beaten jades, just like so many brewers
in their jerkins, made of old boots, riding to fetch in old casks :
and after them as many light-horsemen, with great saddles, and
old broken pistols and scarce a sword among them, just like so
many fiddlers with the fiddles in cases by their horses' sides."
Very little of the pomp and majesty of war about these rough
soldiers! But then we must remember that uniform was not much
in evidence during the earlier stages of the Civil War. According
to the best authorities, the soldiers on either side were clad in all
the colours of the rainbow, according to the fancy of the
Commanding Officer. Thus, on the King's side we read of the
Yellow Regiment, the Red Regiment, the White Coats, the Blacks,
and the Greens. While on the other side there were the six
regiments of London Train-Bands, known as the Yellow, Blue,
Red, White, Green, and Orange. The confusion that was likely
to arise in battle from such a strange medley, even when the
regimental colours were not hidden by great-coats and armour, was
avoided by the wearing of scarves of a uniform colour throughout
each army. Nevertheless we have Cromwell complaining that
"diversity of clothing" led, not infrequently, to the "slaying of

friends by friends." Curiously enough, our national scarlet was the chosen uniform of the rebel army when, in the autumn of 1644, the Parliament decided to adopt a uniform for their soldiers, and a "correspondent" who visited Fairfax's army, in April, 1645, thus described its appearance :—"The men are all Redcoats, all the whole army, only are distinguished by the several facings of their coats. The Firelocks only are some of them tawny coats."*

The day following the capitulation, viz., Monday, Sept. 2nd, King Charles returned to his snug quarters at Boconnoc, glad, no doubt, to get back to a warm bed and regular meals, after roughing it for two days and nights in the open. To quote Symonds : "Tuesday, 3 Sep.—The King and all his army rested—we at Lanreth." His quiet was not of long duration. The "Politic contrivers " were at their evil work again. "The fear and apprehension of the enemy was no sooner over," says Clarendon, "than the murmur began that the King had been persuaded to grant too good conditions to that body of foot ; " which ought, on the contrary, to have been made prisoners of war, thus preventing Parliament from so soon raising another army. How the perennial human nature crops out in all this ! Was there ever a body of officers got together who did not know better what to do than the General in command ? "But they who undertook to censure that action," says Clarendon, " did not at all understand the present temper and constitution of the King's army "—to say nothing of the incompetence of his commanders ; and the historian goes on to point out that the strength and condition of the Royalists were very much over-rated, and that, however efficient and numerous the army may have been on its first entry into Cornwall, a great change for the worse had taken place in the interim—that, in fact, while the articles of capitulation were being settled, the balance of numbers was decidedly in the enemy's favour, who, had they been well informed of the disposition of the King's horse at the time, might very well have broken through the King's lines, at the same time as their horse did, adding that "the King's army in the condition and state it was in, naked and unshod, would, through those

See Note 3.

enclosed parts, narrow lanes, and deep ditches, have been able to do them very little harm."

The campaign being over, there was nothing for it but to get back home again. To quote the diary : " Wednesday, 4.—The King marched from Boconnock to Liskerd ; his Majestie lay at Mr. Jeans. The troops of Life Guards marched six miles further to South Hill." And here we must leave our pleasant companion to seek pastures new and fresh fields of glory or disaster, as he followed the waning fortunes of the King.

Of poor Charles, suffice it to say that he was not fated long to enjoy the sweets of victory. Troubles had already broken out in other parts of the realm, which he now hastened to stem, and loyal Cornwall saw him no more.

There are one or two incidents of the campaign that are worth a passing notice, if only as reflecting the spirit of the times. The first one took place near the Druids' Hill, at Boconnoc, while the Parliamentary troops were being driven back on Lostwithiel. It appears, from the chronicles of the period, that a challenge having been given by a hundred young troopers of the Parliamentary army, of from sixteen to twenty years of age, led on by a Colonel Straughan, who is said to have fought with nothing on but a hat and a shirt, the offer of defiance was accepted in sight of both armies, by Colonel Digby, and a like number of troops on the King's side; but, " being urged by a rash impetuosity, and discharging their pistols at too great a distance," the young Royalists were soon overpowered ; many were thrust through in the conflict, one being half killed on the spot, and none escaping without injury. As the losses of the other side are not reported, we may assume that the account is from a rebel source ; the Royalist version of the affair has yet to be heard.

For an account of the other occurrences we are indebted once more to the Royalist officer, Symonds. Referring to the behaviour of the rebels, he says : " One of their actions while they were at Listithiel must not be forgotten. In contempt of Christianity, Religion, and the Church, they brought a horse to the font in the church, and there, with their kind of ceremonies, did, as they called it, christen the horse, and called him by the name of Charles, in contempt of his sacred Majestie."

Thus did these rude soldiers seek to beguile the tedium of the campaign! A sad foretaste of what was in store for ecclesiastical edifices in other parts of the land! "Another was done by their Provost Martial," says our authority. It appears that the rebels, being hard put to for a lock-up, confined their prisoners in the church; but the night they marched away, two of the prisoners, "being rich men of Cornwall, gott up in the steeple, and pulled up the ladder, and called to the Marshall, jeering at him." This was too much even for that high official. "I'le fetch you down," said he, and, being in a hurry to get off, "sett mulch and hay on fire, under them; besides they shott many muskets into the belfry at them." Still the defiant prisoners stuck to their post. "All would not doe. Then he fetcht a barrel of powder and gave fire to it, threatening to blow them up, and that blew into the church and blew off most of the slate, and yet did no hurt to the prisoners." The sequel is unknown. No wonder after this that the Listithiel folk "had their pennyworths" out of the varlets when the chance offered!

⟶❄ Chapter VI. ❄⟵

The Sequel.

AND thus, for the second time, was King Charles indebted to the loyalty of the Cornish for the successful frustration of the attempt of Parliament to excite rebellion in the West. It was just a year since he addressed to them that letter of heartfelt thanks, which by his direction was copied and placed in a conspicuous part of all their churches, and may even now be read in many of the older ones—"a most honourable monument of their virtues and his gratitude." The letter runs as follows :—

C.R.

To the Inhabitants of the County of Cornwall.

————

We are so highly sensible of the merits of our County of Cornwall, for their zeal for the defence of our person, and the just rights of our crown, in a time when we could contribute so little to our defence, or to their assistance ; in a time when, not only no reward appeared, but great and probable dangers were threatened to obedience and loyalty ; of their great and eminent courage and patience in their indefatigable prosecution of their great work against so potent an enemy, backed with so strong, rich, and populous cities, and so plentifully furnished and supplied with men, arms, money, ammunition, and provision of all kinds ; and of the wonderful success with which it pleased Almighty God (though with the loss of some most eminent persons, who shall never be forgotten by us) to reward their loyalty and patience by many strange victories over their and our enemies in despight of all human probability, and all imaginable disadvantages ; that as we cannot be forgetful of so great desert, so we cannot but desire to publish it to all the world, and perpetuate to all time, the memory of their merits, and of our acceptance of the same; and to that end, we do hereby render our Royal thanks to that our county, in the most public and lasting manner we can devise, commanding copies hereof to be printed and published, and one of them to be read in every church and chapel therein, and to be kept for ever as a record in the same : that as long as the history of these times and of this nation shall continue, the memory of how much that county hath merited from us and our crown, may be derived with it to posterity.

Given at our camp at Sudeley Castle, the 10th of September, 1643.

This expression of "our Royal thanks" has surely a melancholy pathos when studied in the light of after events. Who shall say they were not well deserved? "Nowhere," says the historian, "was the Royal cause to take so brave or noble a form as amongst the Cornishmen;" and he goes on to explain why. "Cornwall stood apart from the general life of England. Cut off from it, not only by differences of blood and speech, but by the feudal tendencies of its people, who clung with a Celtic loyalty to their local chieftains, and suffered their fidelity to the crown to determine their own." And when, contrary to their most earnest supplications, the tide of war was rolled westward, and broke across the Tamar side, they never hesitated in their duty. A little band of brave men at once rallied round the chivalrous Sir Bevil Grenville, "so destitute of provisions that the best officers had but a biscuit a day, and with only a handful of powder for the whole force." Yet this little band of Cornishmen climbed Stratton Hill, and sent the soldiers of the Parliament reeling back across the border; shewing "to all time" how bravely a mere handful of undisciplined countrymen can fight, when animated by a right spirit.

Charles' words seem to well up out of a full heart and appeal to us, across those two and a half centuries, with a force of their own, touching a sympathetic chord in our hearts which not all his perverseness and wrong-doing can entirely deaden.

Appropriately enough, a copy of the letter is affixed to the church at Fowey; for its inhabitants had bitter experience of a Parliamentary occupation; while the surrounding gentry contributed generously to the King's "sinews of war."

A ghastly reminder of these troublous times was brought to

light during the present century, in the course of restoring a noble
house, where a secret chamber was broken into, and the figure of
a man discovered, seated at a table, in the dress of his day.
Bricked up and forgotten, this poor fugitive must have died a
horrible death.   Tradition points to a well-known Royalist, of
good family, who was "wanted" by Essex, as the probable victim.

And thus, having completed our narative, there now only
remains the task of considering the lessons, if any, which the
story of the campaign may seem to convey.   From a strictly
military standpoint, there may not be many valuable lessons to be
gathered, whether in the matter of tactics, or "fire-discipline," or
in the hundred and one technical points that are engaging the
attention of scientific experts at the present time.   It seems a far
cry from these days of competitive examinations and army-
crammers, and wars waged on "scientific principles," to the rough-
and-tumble scrimmages of the Civil War, and the professional
man will probably turn up his nose at the suggestion of there
being anything to be learned from a study of it.   Nevertheless, he
must be a dull witted person that cannot carry away some useful
lesson from the story : for, when we get behind the scenes, or
rather, perhaps, the conventional phraseology of school historians,
we find that men fought and ran away, and performed feats of
splendid heroism, or acts of mean cowardice, just as men do at
the present day, when brought face to face with danger.

What, for instance, were the causes at work which, on the
very eve of the King's victory, brought about the sudden turn of
tide, and set the current strongly against the Royal cause,
gathering volume and force until it overwhelmed King and cause
in one common ruin?   How came it about that the "great army
of rascalls," that pressed all "of a heap like sheep, so dirty and
degraded as was rare to see," past the King, at Castle Dore, were
so quickly reorganized and inspirited as to be able to face him
again next month at Newbury, and recapture the guns they had
surrendered in Cornwall ?

Sir Walter Scott, speaking of these very men (the trained
bands of London), tells us "they were the subject of ridicule in
all the plays and poems of the period."

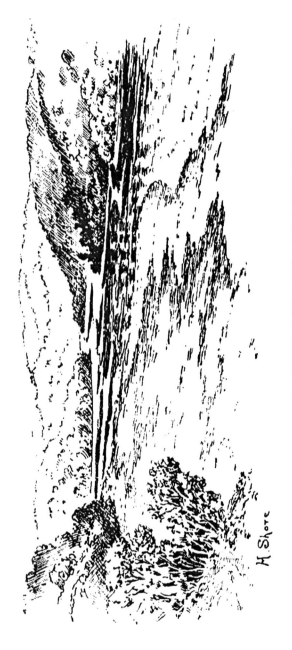

THE RIVER OPPOSITE GOLANT, AT LOW TIDE.

Some clue to these problems may be found in an address delivered some thirteen years later, by Cromwell, to the Parliamentary Commissioners (1657). "On my first going out into this engagement," said that remarkable man, "I saw our men were beaten at every hand, and I desired him (John Hampden) that he would make some additions to my Lord Essex's army of some new regiments. And I told him I would be serviceable to him in bringing such men in as I thought had a spirit that would do something in the work. 'Your troops,' said I, 'are most of them old decayed serving men and tapsters, and such kind of fellows : and their troops are gentleman's sons, younger sons, and persons of quality. Do you think that the spirits of such mean and base fellows will ever be able to encounter gentlemen that have honour, and courage and resolution in them? You must get men of a spirit that is likely to go on as far as gentlemen will go, or else you will be beaten still."

Here, then, we have held up to admiration the very characteristics which have ever distinguished the British officer—characteristics, too, which, in spite of the levelling tendencies of modern times, are still regarded by the most competent judges to be those best calculated to ensure successful leadership at the present day—"gentlemen that have honour, courage, and resolution in them." Now, opinions such as these, coming straight from the lips of one of the greatest men of any age or country—a man who had not only commanded for many years the most formidable instrument for war that, in the opinion of competent judges,* was ever got together on English soil, but who was, perhaps, the most successful leader of men that we have ever produced—are certainly remarkable.

Having thus given credit in the most handsome manner to the qualities which had conduced to the success of the Royalists, Cromwell goes on to point out that it was only possible to meet them with any hope of victory by attracting to the Parliamentary ranks men who were actuated by loftier motives than were their opponents. "I raised such men," said he, "as had the fear of God in before them, as made some conscience of what they did : and from that day forward, I must say to you they were never beaten, and wherever they were engaged against the enemy, they beat continually."

"With his men," says Burnett, "discipline, prompt obedience, endurance, and self-reliance were conspicuous : they were sober, intelligent, devoted to their leaders and their cause—in the fight firm as rocks, never being carried away by success, and in defeat they rapidly rallied and re-formed." And then, when all was over and the mighty instrument by which such great results had been attained was to be thrust aside, Macaulay tells us that "fifty thousand men accustomed to the profession of arms were at once thrown on the world, and experience seemed to warrant the belief that the change would produce much misery and crime, that the discharged veterans would be seen begging in every street, or that they would be driven by hunger to pillage. But no such result followed. In a few months there remained not a trace indicating that the most formidable army in the world had just been absorbed into the mass of the community. The Royalists themselves confessed that in every department of honest labour, the discarded warriors prospered beyond other men, that none was charged with any theft or robbery, that none was heard to ask an alms*, and that if a baker, a mason, or a waggoner attracted notice by his diligence or sobriety, he was in all probability one of Cromwell's old soldiers."

Now, whatsoever opinions may be held as to Cromwell's sincerity or as to the merit of his achievements, there can be no question as to the abilities of the man who could mould the dirty dejected rabble that shambled past King Charles at Castle Dore into the splendid force so justly admired by Macaulay. The man who could achieve such a result must indeed have been endowed with a master-mind.

Such are some of the thoughts conjured up during a ramble over this classic ground, where, as was said, the face of nature has been less altered by the hand of man than in other parts of our island.† The visitor may still stand on the bridge at Lostwithiel over which the armies crossed, and gaze at the very

* This, alas, can hardly be affirmed of our modern systems.
† See Note 5.

church wherein were perpetrated those acts of sacrilege which disgraced the troops of Essex, or he may wander over the " old double-trenched fort" mentioned by Symonds, " wherein the rebels had planted many of their great pieces," possibly even be shown some relics ploughed up from the adjoining fields, and look down from there on to Par, where the supplies for Essex's army were landed, and on the other side to the " pass at St. Veep." He may even try and picture the " rebel horse " plunging across the river below, at low tide, on that foggy September morning in the year 1644, while Goring was sleeping off the effects of his " jovial exercises." While at Fowey, where " the wounded laye,"* he may cross over to the Hall walk and examine the positions " gotten by the vigilant care of Sir Jacob Astley." And then as he bids farewell to these scenes, and, perchance compares the present with the past, he will probably find consolation in the thought that the days of civil war are over, and that his lot has been cast in quieter and happier times.

* See Note 6.

NOTE 1.—It is not generally known how narrowly that venerable structure, Lostwithiel Bridge, escaped destruction on this occasion. According to Clarendon, Essex actually gave orders to break down the bridge to check pursuit : " But his Majesty himself, from his new fort dis-cerned it, and sent a company of musqueteers, who quickly beat those that were left, and thereby preserved the bridge, over which the King presently marched to overtake the rear of the army." For an interesting account of this ancient relic and its historical associations, see a pamphlet entitled " Lostwithiel Bridge and its Memories," by Rev. Canon E. Boger, M.A. 1887.

NOTE 2.—Our English hedge-rows, according to the author of " Words and Places," are the oldest landmarks we have ; so that, were the needful data available, we might identify each spot referred to in the Diary. Even as it is, the thought that these boundaries were coeval with the events described is very suggestive.

NOTE 3.—The following were the words of command in the Parliamentary army for priming, loading, and firing in the ranks :—

1. Balance your musket in left hand.
2. Find out your charge.
3. Open your charge.
4. Charge with bullet.
5. Put your scouring stick in your musket.
6. Ram home your charge.
7. Draw forth your scouring stick.
8. Turn and shorten him to a handful.
9. Return your scouring stick.
10. Bring forward your musket and poize.
11. Balance your musket in left hand with barrel upward.
12. Draw forth your match.
13. Blow the ashes from your coal.
14. Present upon your left hand.
15. Give fire breast high.

NOTE 4.—" He (Cromwell) had the finest army—in fact the only really great army we ever had in England. I think the number was 80,000 men, though the population then was a very small one."—Lord Wolseley's evidence before Lord Wantage's Committee (June, July, 1891).

NOTE 5.—Time has swept away nearly all traces of the Civil War, hereabouts ; but the site of the battery thrown up by the Royalists, on the hill overlooking Lostwithiel, may still be traced, under the title of " King Charles' Redoubt." Many relics of those days have, however, been turned up by the plough from time to time, such as pistols, swords, cannon balls, and bullets. But unquestionably the most interesting memento is the King's Cup, in the possession of R. Foster, Esq., of Lanwithan, near Lostwithiel. This unique relic, which is of silver, measuring 6in. high by 3 across, was presented, so tradition affirms, by the King, in person, on the field of Castle Dore, to a yeoman named Stephens, for raising a troop of horse for the King's service. After being handed down in the family for several generations, it was at length sold, the then owner being a pauper. The original recipient lies buried in St. Winnow Churchyard ; his tomb bespeaks a person of position and property.

NOTE 6.—A letter from Essex contains the following :—" We have sick men sent hither, who, if not timely sent, do die soon after they come here, fresh diet being their only cure. The chirurgeons of the Army are ill stored with provisions, some not having to the value of 10s."

PRINTED BY THE CLEVEDON PRINTING CO. (LTD.)

OLD FOYE DAYS.

PART II.

CONTAINING

An Authentic Account of the Exploits of the Smugglers in and around the Port of Fowey.

Compiled from various sources

BY

Commander Honble. HENRY N. SHORE, R.N.,

AUTHOR OF

"The Flight of the Lapwing in China and Japan,"
"Smuggling Days and Smuggling Ways,"
"Three Pleasant Springs in Portugal,"
ETC., ETC.

———— ————

"*All the labour of man is for his mouth, and yet the appetite is not filled.*" —Ecclesiastes.

1907.

INTRODUCTORY.

"An intimate knowledge of the domestic history of nations is absolutely necessary to the prognosis of political events."—*Macaulay*.

CONTENTS.

INTRODUCTORY.

≈≈≈≈≈

The story of an outrage—A great book-burning—Where are the records?—A human document—The Custom's staff—Principal inhabitants—Lieutenant Bray of the Hinde—The Lottery of Polperro—Where were the Magistrates?—Busy free-traders—A tobacco voyage—Sources of inspiration— Explanatory.

SOME time during the third quarter of the 19th century— the precise date is immaterial—an outrage of a very heinous nature was perpetrated, all unknown to the world, in the ancient port of Fowey. Nay, if tradition is to be relied on, the first, and indeed the only intimation conveyed to the inhabitants of what was happening in their midst, reached them through the olfactory organs :—though, alas! without exciting the least suspicion as to the cause.

It all came about in this wise. Her Majesty's advisers, in their wisdom, and zeal for economy, having seen fit to effect certain reductions in the Custom's department, singled out, amongst other place, the port of Fowey—famed in song and story—as a field for their enterprise; and despatched a pair of sprightly gentlemen from London to give effect to their resolution.

Now, the reception that would have been accorded these emissaries in the good old times, when red-hot zeal for the honour of their town was a marked trait of all good Foyens, may be surmised from the ear-cropping exploits that figure in the civic annals. But we have fallen on degenerate days: and so, these young Londoners— their mission being unsuspected, were not only peaceably admitted, but snugly installed for several days in that noble edifice which, in this venerable sea-port, fulfills the *rôle* of

Custom-house—wherein, as it afterwards came to light, were performed the sacrificial rites pertaining to the solemn function deputed to them.

The precise ceremonial observed on this occasion was never divulged. All that ever leaked out was a strong smell of burning —what an esteemed resident described as a "div'le of a stink," which pervaded the vicinity of the said temple while the observances were in progress. It is common knowledge, however, that the rites took the form of a bonfire, whereby vast quantities of books and papers—the accumulation of centuries, pertaining to the Fowey Customs, were consumed, and their ashes afterwards committed to the deep :—an act of sacrilege by which several hundred-weights of invaluable material for the compilation of history were consigned to an undeserved oblivion.

This great book-burning was consummated, partly on the beach, and partly in a cellar beneath the old mansion abutting on the Custom-house, at that time occupied by Dr. Davis, but since converted into a bank, whose quaint facade, with its beautiful porch, once formed quite the most picturesque feature of the town. And the evil deed completed, the perpetrators thereof returned to London, carrying along with them a parcel of selected documents whose resting-place is not even known. •

It is as useless crying over burnt paper as over spilt milk. Nevertheless, in view of the extreme antiquity of the port of Fowey —whose Customs' records are known to have extended back for several generations, an expression of regret that the fanatics who initiated this piece of vandalism had not the decency to consult the city fathers before completing it, is surely permissible.

From that regretable holocaust but one volume of any value remains—the "Oath Book," to wit: wherein every member of the Customs' staff was wont to record a solemn asseveration touching the faithful performance of his duty. The earliest entry in this "human document" runs as follows :—

"Jan. 3, 1681. This Port of ffowy.

Item. I. Chas Polkinhorne of Helston in the County of Cornwall do sware that I will be faithfull and just to her Maj^ty

in the execution of the Trust in me reposed as Commander
of the Fowye Smack on the account of ye Customs. So
Help me God. Charles. Cha. Polkinhorne. Am be. Coll.
Sworn before us This 22nd of March

Wm. Toller D : Compt."

There follow, also, the declarations of J. Oliver Johns, waiter
and Searcher att Bodinick : and of Thomas Smyth, of Polruan,
Augt. 18th. 1684.

Also of

" The 29th of Octob. 1698.

J. Roger Langon wait^r and Search^r att the Parr. doo swear to
God trew and faithfull in ye execution and discharge to y^e
best of my knowledge and power in the severall trusts and
Imployments committed to my charge and Inspections in
ye service of his Maj^ties Customs. soe help mee God :

Juravit Coram ·   Roger Langdon.
John Dagge Coll^t.
Henry Stephens D. Comp^t."

From a DIRECTORY for the year 1791, we learn that the
Customs' staff was then composed as follows :—

W. Cotton—Surveyor of the Customs and Alderman.
H. Couche—Controller of the Customs.
J. Courts—Collector of the Customs and Alderman.
With 3 Custom-house officers ; 1 Land-waiter ; 3 Salt-officers ; 1
Searcher of salt ; and 1 Excise-officer.

The rapid decline of the port of Fowey, from a Customs
point of view, during the last century, may be gathered from the
following table of " Securities " required from the Collectors of
Customs :—

1830	...	...	...	...	...	£4,000
1840	...	...	...	...	...	3,000
1845	...	...	...	...	...	2,000
1850	...	...	...	...	...	1,500
1881	...	...	...	...	...	500

From a " List of the principal inhabitants," of the same date,
we learn that the town supported no less that 3 Surgeons, 2 Attor-

neys, 1 Innkeeper, 4 Ship-builders, 1 Musician, and a Peruke-maker. There were also no fewer than 13 resident Naval Officers, comprising 2 Captains, 5 Lieutenants, 2 Masters, and a Purser. Of the Lieutenants, one was employed on the " Impress Service," while another—Lieut. Gabriel Bray, earned some notoriety, eight years later, when in command of the Revenue Cutter Hinde, 160 tons, 16 guns, and 24 men, by the capture of the famous smuggling vessel, " Lottery," of Polperro, off the Lizard, after a 14-hours' chase, on the morning of May 14, 1799. The crew of this notorious craft had been " wanted " for several months past in connection with the murder of a Revenue officer on the night of Dec. 26, 1798, off Penlee Point, near Cawsand.

The " Lottery affair " created a good deal of excitement at the time, and together with its tragic sequel has been immortalised by Mr. Jonathan Couch in his " HISTORY OF POLPERRO." The story—full of inaccuracies as it is, contains all the elements of a thrilling romance, and the materials have been skilfully utilised by a talented authoress in a picture of Polperro life, entitled " Adam and Eve." (By Mrs. Parr.)*.

Coming to later times, we find a Lieut. Burn in charge of the Sea-Fencibles, here, from 1807, till the reduction of the corps in 1811. While, from other sources we find mention of the Snow, " Jobson of Fowey,"—owners Thomas Slade and Thomas Cogan, as being granted a pass for the Mediterranean. (June, 1815.) And during the same year the Commander of the " Providence " Revenue Cruiser, reports that having taken some smugglers in the open boat, " James and Mary," in Fowey harbour, and there being no Justice of the Peace at Fowey, the men were taken to Plymouth.

A reference to the Customs' " Oaths of admission " book shows that the following were Justices of the Peace at Fowey at the dates named :—1821, Robert Hearle and R. S. Flamank ;

---

* A detailed account of this famous affair, compiled from authentic sources, was contributed by the present writer to the *Western Morning News*, under the title, " A POLPERRO TRAGEDY ; OR, THE TRUE STORY OF THE LOTTERY " (April 5th and 8th, 1905).

1826, Robert Hearle, Mayor; John Bennet, Justice; 1827, John Kempe, Justice.

From documents in the Record Office, and elsewhere, we obtain evidence of the commercial enterprise of the Foyens, thus:—

1824.—The "Elizabeth" and "Grace," of Fowey, are caught smuggling.

1829.—The "Lucy," of Fowey, is seized, in January, at Chichester, with concealments containing 100 half-ankers of spirits on board.

1832.—The "Rose" sailed from Roscoff with 100 tubs of brandy for Fowey. Also, the following vessels were reported at Roscoff taking in cargoes:—The "Eagle," 35 tons, and the "Rose," 11 tons, both of Fowey and for Fowey. And again, later, the "Eagle" sailed from Roscoff with 300 tubs for the Fowey district; followed soon after by another trip with 150 tubs for the Fowey district. And the following year a "well-informed correspondent" reports from Roscoff that the "Eagle," on board which are the two Dunstans from Portloe, "has been very success- ful; she sailed on the 27th March, landed her cargo, and was back at Roscoff on the 31st. A tobacco voyage will now take place: Mallaby is conducting the operations with the greatest secrecy, and is trying to get authorized by the Customs to load in the roads of the Isle of Bas."

The "Love," also, is reported as sailing with 150 tubs for Fowey.

In 1833, two men belonging to Fowey, and one from Pol- ruan, serving in the Coastguard, are dismissed for being con- cerned in some smuggling transaction.

But these dry, official jottings convey a sadly inadequate idea of the zeal and enterprise with which the inhabitants of Fowey and the adjacent country carried on the "free-trade," or, as we call it nowadays, "smuggling." "He who wishes to understand the condition of man in former ages," says Macaulay, "must mingle in the crowd. He must obtain admission to the convivial table and the domestic hearth. He must bear with vulgar expres-

sion, and not shrink from exploring even the retreats of misery."
In short, we must seek elsewhere for inspiration if we would
master the ins and outs of the smuggling industry.

Now, it so chanced that it was the writer's good fortune, in
days gone by, to hold a Coastguard appointment at the port of
Fowey; which comprised the supervision of several miles of the
adjacent coast. And with a view to qualifying as an efficient protector of the revenue, and, at the same time, satisfying his own
unbounded curiosity, he sought out and became acquainted with
every old person who had been in any way concerned with the
introduction, through illicit channels, of the good and bad
spirits, which the Cornishmen of former days loved, not always
wisely, but too well. Following Macaulay's advice, he pushed
his quest into all sorts of unorthodox channels, thus unearthing
quite a number of "ancients" of either sex, who, when tactfully
approached, proved very ready to disclose, not only those curious
details which fall under the heading of "trade secrets," but such
experiences as had fallen to their particular lot. And from the
lips of these Cornish worthies a very plethora of information relating to the now lost art of smuggling was slowly extracted.

Obviously it would have been injudicious to have imparted
these confessions to the world during the lifetime of the estimable
folk who had thus obligingly unloaded their consciences. And,
even now, long after all who could speak from personal experience
of the trade have joined the great migration, some little diffidence
is felt as to the propriety of making them public. Indeed, it is
only at the urgent solicitation of a very dear and valued friend,
in whose literary taste and sound judgment the writer has the
most implicit trust—the newspaper boy, to wit—that these pages
are now sent forth, with all apologies for their imperfections, and
the fervent hope that the perusal of their contents may conduce
to a better appreciation of a once great and prosperous industry.

THE POSTHUMOUS PAPERS

OF

THE POLRUAN

MUTUAL IMPROVEMENT SOCIETY

(LIMITED).

———

"Relations of matter of fact have a value from their substance as much as from their form, and the variety of events is seldom without entertainment or instruction, however indifferently soever the tale is told."—*Sir Wm. Temple.*

EXPLANATORY.

Though lost to sight, to memory dear—An unknown Boswell—
   Honeymooning in Eden—Truth stranger than fiction—A
   curious coincidence—The question of dates—Coy smugglers
   —Pontius Pilate at Polruan—The perfect historian.

AN old monk, so the story runs, on being questioned about
   certain monastic documents, cloaked his ignorance by re-
   plying that they were "mysteries of the church." The
answer served its purpose, and I must warn my readers that an
equally evasive reply awaits any too-curious student who would
fain pry into the antecedents of the following records.

That the POLRUAN MUTUAL IMPROVEMENT SOCIETY
(LIMITED), came into being, that it enjoyed a useful,
if all too brief, career, and that it fell into dissolution ere ever the
world had come to realise its existence, is all that really need be
known about it. To be sure, that vigilant watch-dog, the contemporary press, may be searched in vain for any allusion to the
Society. But have not some of the most momentous revolutions
in the world's history been hatched in the quietude of a back
parlour? And does not our greatest historian tell us that "the
circumstances which have most influenced the happiness of mankind have been, for the most part, noiseless revolutions?"

That the Society had the good fortune to produce a Boswell
is manifest from the existence of its records. And albeit nothing definite is known concerning the birth-place and manner-
of-life of this worthy soul, that he was no Cornishman must be
patent to every native of the Duchy, who, as he devours these
pages, will ofttimes be moved to mirth at the chronicler's futile

attempts to give expression to the colloquialisms which render
"Cornish as she is spoke"—according to the modern novelist,
so much more adequate a vehicle for the materialisation of thought
than the mutilated English of the Board Schools.

But how did these treasures find their way into the editor's
hands? Neither wild horses, nor tame asses, shall drag that
secret from his breast. If that lying jade, rumour, is to be trusted
for once, the penalties attaching to any breach of confidence on
the part of a sworn member of the Society were almost terrifying
in their severity. The editor's reluctance, therefore, to furnish
any clue to the identity of his informant will be readily understood.

But why worry over the matter? Enquiries into the origin of
things invariably land us in the primeval slime, where the wise
and the foolish, alike, slither about without touching bottom.
When our lightly attired ancestors were honeymooning in Eden,
and Adam received that fateful apple at the hands of his spouse—
most delectable of travelling companions, unencumbered with
jewel-case, or even trousseau— did he stop to enquire about its
antecedents? No; he just gobbled it up—too greedily for the
happiness of the human race, alas! confiding in the wisdom of
his partner's choice; and, lo! his eyes were opened. And if the
reader will just be content to swallow the historic fragments herein offered in the same trustful spirit, his eyes will be opened too,
and he will begin to perceive, in spite of all he learnt in the
vulgar tongue at the instance of his god-parents, his own intellectual nakedness in respect of a branch of industry which
monopolised the time and thoughts of thousands of earnest, God-
fearing Cornishmen in times past. In short, a careful study of
these pages will afford one more proof of the truth of Shakes-
pear's remark :—

"There are more things in heaven and earth, Horatio,
  Than are dreamt of in your philosophy."

But what guarantee have we of their authenticity? For,
alas! it must be confessed there have been people rash enough
to insinuate doubts touching their bona-fides. But, then, did not
a learned Divine once compile a treatise to prove that there never

had been, and never could have been, such a person as Napoleon Buonaparte? How then could the P.M.I. Society, Ltd., expect immunity from the attacks of sceptics? Let me, therefore, explain that when these archives passed into my hands there were people still living who could speak from personal knowledge of the events therein recorded, and whose testimony so exactly agreed with the written narrative that but one inference was possible, namely, that the personal experiences of these veterans formed the subject matter of the records. And when, in due course, the names of these makers of history, whose friendship it was the writer's privilege to enjoy, were discovered figuring in the official records of the Coastguard service, and in connection with the identical occurrences they had so graphically described, this inference at once ripened into conviction. From that moment all doubts concerning the bona-fides of the documents vanished, and the editor at once realised the unique character of his possession.

There still remained the question of dates. It was felt that such definitions of time as " back-along," or " when I was sarvin' along wi' Mr. Hicks up to Tregabrown," or " time Billy Hocken kept the Red Heifer public-house," though expressive in their way, were hardly precise enough to satisfy the requirements of historical exegesis. But where to turn for the needful information? There was the rub. Neither Municipal archives; nor Parish Registers; nor Episcopal Charges; nor Parochial Histories help one in any way. Indeed, the lack of attention displayed by " sober historians " to the principles and practices of an industry which once exercised a profound influence on the happiness of mankind, is simply scandalous. True, the omission may be attributed, in no small degree, to the well-known aversion of all great captains of industry to publicity. For, strange as it may seem, in these hustling, self-advertising days, the really capable smugglers were excessively coy of seeing their exploits in print. Like true heroes, they affected a quite remarkable reticence in regard to their own share in the making of history. Nor was it then etiquette to furnish " copy " to the press, or even to

·

invite "our local correspondent" to assist at a run of goods. Of
course, the world is the poorer for this. Just consider, for example, what masterpieces a Stevens, or a Kipling, or even a Marie
Corelli would have dashed off, had these giants of literature been
privileged to witness a landing of good spirits in the old style!
So stirring a theme would have awakened the muse of the Poet
Laureate, to say nothing of minor warblers.

But to get back to the dates. And first, as regards the incu-
bation of the Society. Judging from internal evidence, the editor
is inclined to locate this epoch-making event somewhere between
the years 1870-80. It is on record, moreover, that at about this
period a wave of intellectual activity swept over Polruan. The
spirit of inquiry simply raged through the place, and presently
assumed material form in that imposing institution for the study
of A, B, C, which, in company with St. Saviour's chapel and the
Coastguard look-out house, crowns the hill, and by reason of its
noble proportions and fine architecture, challenges the attention
of visitors.

The beneficient results that have flowed from this great centre
of learning are so well known that to dilate on them further would
merely weary the reader. Let the following example suffice. A
young lady, aged 12, holding a post in a private household, com-
bining hard work with modest remuneration, on being asked the
purpose of the famous beacon at the harbour's mouth—commonly called "Punch's Cross," promptly replied that it had been
placed there by Pontius Pilate. Truly, the schoolmaster has not
laboured all these years in vain.

As regards the dates of the several events described in the
chronicles, it has been possible, by dint of much quarrying amidst
mountains of irrelevant matter, to fix the times of all the most important ones, and, further, by supplementing the narrative by extracts from official records, greatly to enhance its value.

It is just possible, of course, that the full significance of these
chronicles of a vanished past may not be appreciated all at once.
Nay, in some minds there may even spring up a feeling of resent-
ment at being introduced to such low company, or at the imperti-

nence of a mere alien in raking up the heroic achievements of
" Former men in Far Cornwall." But does not a justly-admired
writer tell us that " to look back upon what is beginning to appear
almost a fabulous era in the eyes of the modern children of light,
is not unamusing or uninstructive; for, still better to appreciate
the present, we should be led not infrequently to recall the intellectual muzziness of the past?"

" The perfect historian," says a professor of the craft, " is he
who considers no anecdote, no peculiarity of manner, no familiar
saying, as too insignificant for his notice." Let us remember,
moreover, that, to quote the words of a famous philosopher, " All
that we do, all that we are, is the outcome of ages of labour;"
wherein, be it remarked, the smugglers played a much more shin-
ing part than is commonly supposed.

Just another word. The " perfect historian " of the Duchy
has yet to arise. When, however, in his search for material wherewith to compile the economic history of Cornwall during the 19th
century, this peerless scribbler turns to these pages for enlighten-
ment—as assuredly he will, is it too much to ask him to acknow-
ledge the source of his inspiration?

INAUGURATION OF THE SOCIETY.

≋

Local enthusiasm — A treatise on Barnacles—Go it, Cinders!—An
abuse of justice—The town tap—A startling proposal—
Smuggling, falsely so-called—A waste of good liquor—Now,
Jimmy, I've found you!—A question of membership—Good,
staunch chaps.

To evolve a coherent account of the opening ceremony from
the crude mass of undigested notes left by the diarist has been no
easy task. The editor trusts, however, that by the rigid exclusion of
all extraneous matter, and a judicious selection of such details
only as possess historical value, he has compiled a record
worthy of the occasion.

AN event fraught with such important results to the town as
the formation of a Mutual Improvement Society caused
quite a little flutter of excitement. Every branch of local
trade and industry was represented. Even the Sanitary authorities sent their deputy, in the person of the Dustman: while
educational enthusiasts, and people interested in good works, displayed a warm sympathy with the movement. The greatest enthusiasm, however, was manifested by the young folk—boys and
girls alike—who formed quite a crowd long before the time fixed
for the opening of the doors, and presently, in default of admission, gave vent to their feelings in those bizarre manifestations so
beloved of youth.

The meeting had scarcely settled to business and the election
of a chairman when the rift within the lute began to manifest itself. One of the most respected residents—Captain Stockhollum,

whose Treatise on " The cultivation of barnacles on ships' bottoms with a view to the improvement of seamen's dietary on long voyages "—caused such a flutter in scientific circles some years ago, having suggested marine zoology as a fit subject for inquiry, the representative of sanitation jumped up, with the peculiar alertness begotten of long practice in getting on and off a cart-shaft, and declared, somewhat acrimoniously, that the object of the Society was the improvement of the mind, and, if the Captain wanted to talk about " hinsects—leastways he took it that was what the Cap'n was driving at—he had come to the wrong shop, and . . ." The rest of the speech was lost in the uproar caused by a voice from the back calling out, " Go it, Cinders !"

Order having been restored, Mr. Zebedee Curl-paper, of the Lanteglos Toilet Club, rose to propose the " Origin of Cornish Cream, especially in relation to its application to 'splits,'" as an interesting subject of research. When up rose the Town Crier's Deputy and said he " took that as pussonal, seein' as how it was well known to every one in Polruan that he had been County-courted for not paying his cream bill ; vich haction," he went on to say, " was a gross abuse of the Royal Courts of Justice, seeing as how he had been laid up for three months with the brown typhus (bronchitis?), thereby losing the emoluments of his office for that time."

The ladies having exhausted their sympathy for this estimable and unmarried public functionary, a gentleman, with a sad cast of countenance, in the front row, proposed " Wesley's work in Cornwall " as a very proper subject for engaging the attention of the Society, especially in view of the young people, whose thoughts would be the better for being directed to serious channels. But, on someone calling out, " He was agin the smugglers," the sad-faced proposer collapsed.

After some further confused talk, an austere dame, wielding an umbrella rather threateningly, suggested that the researches of the Society should be directed towards the discovery of the town's water supply. This gave rise to angry recriminations ; certain people waxing so hot over the matter that the Chairman threatened

to put some of them under the town tap, which happened to be
running at the moment.

The initial excitement having subsided, as shewn by the
diminishing and rather somnolent audience, the question of membership came up for discussion. But here, again, a bone of con-
tention was thrown in by a gentleman, desirous, it was suspected,
of seeing his name in print, moving " that the proceedings of the
Society be communicated to the Press." The motion was instantly quashed however. Whereupon one of the oldest and most
respected inhabitants proposed that, " having regard to the antecedents of the place, and the well-known commercial instincts of
the people, there could be no fitter subject for research than the
history of that particular branch of trade in which so many of
their fellow-townsmen had been interested in times past, when the
liberty of the subject was still held sacred, and no tyrannical
Government had yet dared to interfere with the industries of their
native place." " He referred, of course," the speaker went on to
say, " to that particular branch of commercial enterprise which
had been falsely called ' smuggling.' It was difficult," he continued, in a tremulous voice, " to speak temperately on a subject
once so dear to Cornishmen—a cause in which so many of their
dearest relatives and friends, aye, their own flesh and blood, had
suffered a cruel martyrdom in that emblem of tyranny, the County
Gaol, up Bodmin way. He was sure there were few in the room
'that evening who were not connected in some way with members
of that once flourishing industry who had laid down their lives
in the cause of free-trade, not in fair and open fight with preventive officers, for that would have been a death to glory in, but in
conflict with the elements—the winds and the waves, which had
swallowed up so many lives, aye, and so many cargoes of beautiful French brandy, to say nothing of gin and tobacco. Ah! my
friends," continued the speaker, warming to his subject, " just
think of the waste of good liquor that went on every year in that
bit of green sea 'twixt here and Rusco (Roscoff). Where was the
harm of bringing it across, he would like to know ? Wasn't it all
bought in the open market ? aye, and paid for, too ? Then where
did the smuggling come in ? Didn't——" At this point a shrill

female voice struck in—" Now, Jimmy, I've a found ye at last! A pretty rig you've a led me! You just come home to wanct! D'ye hear? 'Tis bedtime!"

Jimmy having been marched off to bed, and the furtive glances at the door, in trembling expectation of further summonses, having ceased, the last proposal was put to the vote, and carried nem. con.

There now only remained the question of membership, which turned, presently, on the expediency or otherwise of admitting people who had been instrumental, either as principals or agents, in suppressing the trade. The discussion had gone on some time, and was waxing hot, when up jumped Cap'n Stockhollum, of Barnacles fame, and asked, " What for should you want to keep out the preventive men? who, to my knowledge, was good, staunch chaps, and liked a drop of French brandy as well as any one, prowiding and exceptin' always that it hadn't paid tax to the Government, which was all werry right and proper. And, supposing as how they did interfere with lawful trading," continued the Cap'n, " they had to make a living, like anyone else. There was old Richard Kingcup, now, him as wore a Coastguard button one time, and then joined in along with the free-traders . . . ." The peroration was drowned amidst cries of " Dry up, Reuben, my boy, 'tis late!"

After some further wrangling as to whether Magistrates and members of the police force were eligible for membership, and as touching the admission of newspaper reporters to the meetings, to which latter proposal strong objection was taken by a leading educationalist on the ground of what he called the " premature diwulgment" of the Society's proceedings being calculated to interfere with the publication of the official version, the meeting was adjourned.

MEETING THE FIRST.

MEMBERS PRESENT :

Captain Stockhollum.	Author of the celebrated Treatise on Barnacles, and Literary Adviser to the Society.
Zebedee K.	Retired Agriculturist (in receipt of parish relief).
William T.	Formerly a Protector of the Revenue.
Pascoe R.	Merchant of Polruan.
John A.	A Mechanic from Downderry.
Thomas M.	Formerly a Protector of the Revenue.
Isaiah H.	Farmer from Lanreath way.
Reuben C.	Merchant of Polperro.
Jabez S.	Formerly a Protector of the Revenue.

And others.

P. R.—'Twas a crying shame putting down that free-trade! What's your opinion, old man?

Z. K.—Spirits ain't what they was; no, not by a long chalks.

I. H.—If they'd let us alone for another five years I shouldn't have been what I am. Why, I stood to clear £500 on that last venture what was grabbed by them thieving sharks down at Lantic Bay. You can mind that Saturday night, I dessay?

Capt. S.—It's my opinion if they'd sent the Queen a tub of Mallaby's No. 1 brandy, time she was down here, just to let her taste the stuff, and see what good spirits was like, she'd never have let 'un interfere with a trade what was bread-and-butter to many of 'em. Why, 'twas a good living to lots of pore chaps about here, chaps as never done no good at anything else. I suppose you'll remelect the time Her Majesty was here back along?

Z. K.—Recomember it! Why, surely! Didn't my missus say to me, " Bless thee, Zebedee, if the Queen aint a-wearing cotton stockings!" Aye, and the old Squire druv her to Lostwithiel to see a mine, and the chaps as took her down, not knowing who she was, says, " don't ee be afeared, my dear; there ain't nothing to hurt ee!"

I. H.—'Twas a great business that affair at Lantic Bay, what you was talking about, so I've heard tell.

R. C.—A big business! Why, 'twas the heaviest run of goods that ever came off near Fowey, this century, at any rate. There was a pretty passul of men out that night; aye, and 'twas a wonder none of they prewentive chaps got pitched over the cliff!

Z. K.— I spose I know as much of that business as anyone here; so if you'll keep quiet I'll spin you a bit of a yarn about it.

The Fight at Lantic Bay.

'Twas a brave while back, nigh on to 60 years, I should say, some time in March, but I remember it all, just as if 'twas yester-day. I was working for Mr. Hicks, him what had the farm at Tregabrown. 'Twas a Sunday mornin', somewheres about five o'clock I reckon; anyways, I know I was sleeping heavy-like, having a drop of liquor in me, when I was roused by John Ellory, the Gunner of the old Fox—the revenue cutter as lay at Fowey in those days—he and Richard Clemas who was in the Fox along with him. I was living down at Pont then. They came hammer-ing at the door, calling out, " you'm wanted up at the farm to take some tubs into Polruan; so hurry up, old man, and bustle into your breeks!" Oh, thinks I, that's your little game, is it? So I clapt on a bit of clothes and hurried away up, and when I got to the farm I see'd all the Coastguards about—a regular flock of 'em —and they told me the tubs was in a field on top of the hill above the farm. So I gets the horses put to, though 'twarnt barely light, the wagon, too, was a big 'un—what the hay was carried in—and started away up to the brow of the hill, and there the tubs lay, sure 'nuff; a brave lot, too, I can tell ee, all piled up like shot, and some of the smugglers was standing alongside of 'em.

I. H.—See me there, old man?

Z. K.—Ees, I should think I did, with a hole in the starn of your breeks big enough to clap a tub in. Well, as I waur saying, we loaded up the wagons—a hunderd and seven tubs, that's what there was, neither more nor less—and a brave show they made, I can tell ee. I wanted to have a sup o' sperits, but I'm danged if they'd let me have even a sniff at un, though I knew there'd been one broached, for I seed the staves laying about, and the Coastguards was reg'lar stinking of the stuff, and no mistake. Well, I started off with the load, and druv the wagon right down to the quay at Polruan; and 'twas a goodish load, too, mind you, for the tubs was piled up just like a lot of hay; but I had a pair of 'osses in the wagon, and they took it down nicely, aye, tubs and all. Some of the Coastguards lent us a hand down Polruan Hill, and when we got to the quay the tubs were clapt into a boat and taken across to the Custom House at Fowey, and I never had a taste; no, dang me if I had! And all the time those Prewentive chaps waur reeking of it!

W. T.—Ye lie, old man.

Z. K.—All right, friend, you'll have your say presently; let me finish mine. But 'tis gospel truth what I say. Where was I? Oh! I mind. Well, as I was going along with the wagon I saw two more tubs lying under the hedge. The Inspecting Commander seed them too, and he sung out, "you come along back for them arterwards." So as soon as I'd brought the wagon home I took the two tubs down on the donkey. There were six men taken along with the tubs, all belonging Lanreath way. They was Tom May, Peter May, and a farm labourer called Giles. I can't rightly call to mind who the others was, though I see'd them all plain enough when they were being taken into Polruan. They were caught like this—oh! it was a stupid business, and no mistake. You see, after they'd got the tubs on top of the hill, above Lantic Bay, the chaps sat down for a spell, and got drinking and yarning, thinking they was safe, I suppose; when all of a sudden the Coastguards and Fox's men came right on top of 'em. If they hadn't behaved foolish-like—drinking and going on so—they'd

have got the goods inland, out of harm's way afore ever the Coastguards got out there. I've heard there was more than a hundred
men out at Lantic that night, and there was some pretty severe
fighting with the Coastguards, leastways so they said. I'd been
out about six o'clock on the Saturday morning looking arter the
sheep, away out to Pencarrow Point, and I see'd the old Fox come
down from the eastward. She stood into the bay a bit, and then
turned out and ran away towards Falmouth. The goods had all
been landed then and stowed away in the cliff, so I've been told,
but I never see'd no men about, though I heard arterwards as how
two of 'em had been hid away in the cliff along with the goods all
day. There's a place as big as a room down there now, where you
could put any number of tubs away and no one would twig
them. So far as I can mind, the tubs was brought over by a Cossand man called Andrews, though I don't know what boat came
across with them; but it's like enough to have been a Cossand
one. There was a pretty lot of smuggling went on along this
coast when I was young. They landed a deal of stuff at Lantivet
Bay, and down at Coombe, under Llansalloes, yonder. There
was a farmer called R——, father of the Doctor what lived at
Fowey, back along, who used to carry on a pretty rig at Trevarder
Farm. Why now, I can mind when a cargo was landed at Lantivet, may be sixty year agone, and hid in the adit of the mine,
where the Coastguard found it on information. Now, I reckon
that lot belonged to Mr. R——, at Trevarder. Then there was a
carpenter, at Lanreath, who did a deal in that line. He never
went across hissel, but got the goods brought over. I can mind,
too, when a cargo was run up to Golant, on the Fowey river—a
brave while back that was—and a Golant man got drinking the
night the stuff was landed, and drank hissel to death. 'Twas a
shameful waste of liquor! Now, that's about all I can tell you.
You know something about the affair at Lantic, Isaiah, I reckon?
so let's hear what you've got to say.

I. H.—Oh, I can mind it well enough, seeing as how my
brother was taken that time. It was a tidy while back, sure 'nuff.
It was about the last big smuggling affair on this coast, not but

what there wasn't a goodish bit of smuggling went on long after,
but it was the last time there was any fighting with the Coastguards. We were living up to Lanreath then; my brother was
'prenticed to a farmer there, and was serving his last year, so he
must have been about twenty at the time he was took.

R. G.—How came he to be out along with the smugglers?

I. H.—Why, 'twas like this: the farmer he was with was
one of the wenturers, and he used to get a good bit of stuff brought
over time and again; and, of course, the wenturers would get
together as many men as they could collect to carry the goods
away after they had been landed. Well, now, I don't doubt but
what Mr. H—— had word that the goods were at Lantic Bay,
so he sent all his chaps down there to lend a hand, and, of course,
my brother went along with them. The Coastguards come on top
of 'em in the middle of it all, and there was some spirited fighting;
leastways five of the chaps was took. There was Peter and
Thomas May—big Tom May, as they called him—Thomas Mar-
tin, Edward Pearn, and my brother. They were all hired bearers,
you must understand—labouring-men, not wenturers. Well,
next morning, that was Sunday, they were taken aboard the Fox,
Revenue cutter, in Fowey harbour, and kept there till the Saturday follerin' when they were taken afore the Magistrates in the
Town Hall, and committed for trial up to Bodmin, where they
were kept in the prison till the Assizes came on. One of the
Magistrates who committed them was the Parson at Lanreath.
They were defended by a clever sort of chap, though he warn't
no lawyer, but a farmer, auctioneer, and parish officer for the
poor at Lanreath; and as he knew the men was 'spectable, and
done nothing but help carry a drop of liquor from the coast for
their masters, and, what's more, had families depending on them,
leastways, most of 'em had, why, of course, he tried hard to get
them off. He knew that if they was convicted the parish would
have to support the families. But it 'twasn't no good, for when
the Magistrates heard who he was they told him to keep silence.
This was at Fowey. After they was committed and sent up to
Bodmin to stand trial, the parson at Lanreath, seeing how things

stood, tried hard to get them free, but he couldn't manage that. 'Twas easy enough, you see, to get them into prison, but it warn't so easy a matter getting them out again. Once in there they had to stick and take their trial. However, they'd scarcely been in a week afore the Assizes came on, and all of 'em was acquitted. My brother went to Australy soon arter, and died there. Now, that's all I can tell you.

Capt. S.—Poor chaps! And I suppose they never got no compensation for the loss of time?

I. H.—Not so much as the price of a glass o' gin!

J. A.—My old dad had a werry narrow squeak of being took that time at Lantic Bay. I wasn't out myself, but I've heard the old man talk about it many a time. He used to say there was some desperate fighting with sticks, aye, and some firing, too, along with the Fox's men. None of 'em was wounded, though several got tidy whacks from the bludgeons. The chaps what was taken was sent up to Bodmin, as Zebedee was saying, and acquitted, because they were charged with felony instead of smuggling. Some of the Coastguards got knocked about with the sticks, d'ye see; so when the jury found them "not guilty" of felony the Judge said he must acquit them, as they weren't charged with smuggling. Old dad was one of the wenturers that time, and before the trial came on he engaged a lawyer chap from Liskeard way, one Benjamin L——, to defend them, and paid him £30 down, the rest being paid by the Company. You See there was a Co. in the business, each one paying share-and-share-alike. L—— got a clever chap to plead for them at the trial, and he managed well by them. Father took jolly good care to keep away from Bodmin while the trial was on; indeed, he told us if the men were convicted he'd have to leave the country. The Company consisted of John N——, Richard J——, C——, and some Cossand chaps; in fact, it was a Cossand affair. I can mind very well when the men came home again after they'd been acquitted. Two or three of them lived about Downderry. The Company had to find all the expenses of the trial, and if the men had been convicted would have had to keep their families all the time they were in prison. Father just saved one tub—a small two-gallon one. You see, he had on a coat with werry large pockets in the tails, and when the scuffle began he clapped the tub into it, and gave leg home as fast as he could pull foot.

Capt. S.—He must have had a tidy walk! Why, it'll be twelve or fourteen mile from Lantic Bay to Downderry!

J. A.—Aye, that's so! But lor bless you, the old man thought nothin' of that. He'd often set off of an evening and not get home again before the morning. You wouldn't get chaps to do that nowadays, I reckon!

R. C.—You'm right, John, I don't know what's come over the young 'uns; they ain't what they was; no, not by a long ways.

Capt. S.—Now, I'm thinking it's time we heard what some of the Prewentive men have to say about that 'ere business.

P. R.—Wait a bit; there's Reuben, let's hear what he's got to say first.

R. C.—Well, t'aint much I can tell ee, for I was but a nipper at the time, living up with the farmer who had Tregabrown; still, I can mind the affair werry well, for the night it came off a lot of men called at the farm after dark—we was all between the blankets—and threw gravel agin the windows to wake us up, I reckon. The old man got out of bed, threw up the window, and asked 'un whatever they wanted at that time of night. They said they wanted to know the way to Lantic Bay. So the old man told them, and they went off; and though he couldn't make out what their game was he thought they must be arter tubs. Next morning—Sunday—there was a pretty to-do. All the carts and horses were called out by the Coastguards to carry the tubs down to Polruan, and when we got up top of the hill, over against Lantic Bay, there was a pretty sight of tubs piled up, just where the Coast guards had come on them while they were having a wet. There was a tidy lot of people about, too, come to see the game; indeed, hardly anyone went to church or chapel that morning in Polruan. A heap of people was down at the quay, too, to see the tubs put in the boat. We had a tidy old job getting the wagon down Polruan Hill, sure 'nuff, full up, as 'twas, though we had lots of help, what with Coastguards and Customs people, and all the Fox's men, too. I remember the prisoners being taken on board the Fox; the only one I knew was a tall chap we called "Big Tom May."

Z. K.—That wasn't the first lot of tubs landed at Lantic Bay; no, not by a long chalks. Indeed, I remember the Coastguards coming once before and searching all over the house at Trega-brown for tubs that had been landed down in the Bay. Well, times is changed, ain't they, old man?

R. C.—That's what my missus said last time we was at a burryin', and there wasn't so much as a toothful of sperrits going round. People ain't so free-living as they was.

Capt. S.—Now, Mr. T——, I'm thinking it's about time we had the official warsion of that there affair down at Lantic. Let's hear what you knows about it.

W. T.—'Twas a tidy while back, but I can remember it, aye, same as if 'twas last week. I was sarvin' in the Fox cutter. We'd been up to the eastward, and, coming back to Fowey, passed Lantic Bay in the first part of the night; leastways, that was my impression, but it may have been in the early morning. Ye see we were always going back'ard and for'd to Plymouth, and it's easy to mistake one time for another. Anyways, we'd no sooner anchored off Polruan than orders came for us to go to Falmouth. Just afore we started I was sent ashore in one of the boats to Pol-ruan, and old Joe Dickney, a farmer and smuggler, as lived in an old house out by Lantivet Bay, who was at the landing, said to me: "Hullo, where be bound this day in sich a wind?" It was blowing werry hard from the eastward, and he'd noticed the sails being hoisted. I says, "Oh, we'm bound down Falmouth." "Oh! Falmouth, be ye." This was just what he wanted to find out; for you see he was in with the "run" at Lantic, and now that he knew the coast would be clear that night he would away and tell the chaps, for the tubs had all been landed. It was be-lieved to have been the "Daniel and William," of Cossand, as brought over the tubs. She wasn't bound for Lantic Bay, mind you; but seeing the Fox running down the coast she slipped in

there and landed her tubs; and on a dark night, with a easterly
wind, a boat could lay in there, under the land, quiet enough, without being seen by anything passing. I always thought that was
the way we missed her; but maybe Zebedee was right, and we
ran past the bay in the morning watch, after the tubs had been
stowed in the cliff. Well, as it happened, we got back to Fowey
that same night, beating up against a strong easterly gale all day,
with three reefs down in the mainsail, and all the boats secured
on deck—old Cap'n Best was a rare hand at driving her against
a heavy sea.* As soon as we dropped anchor in Fowey harbour
—about ten o'clock, me'be—the Coastguard boat from Polruan
came alongside, and told the skipper there was a run coming off
at Lantic Bay, and asked for help. Eleven or twelve men jumped
into the boat with their arms, landed, and scampered off to Lantic as hard as they could pull foot. I was left as ship-keeper,
being a youngster; but, of course, I heard about the affair from
the chaps as went. Mr. Barrett, the riding officer, was in charge,
and when they got to Lantic they heard the smugglers swearing
and calling out to the Coastguards that they wouldn't get any
help from the Fox's that night, thinking she was away at Falmouth. "We defy you!" "We'll get them away all safe!" that's
what they shouted. Mr. Barrett fired his pistol when pretty close
and then there was a bit of a scuffle, and six or seven of the
smugglers were captured and taken aboard the Fox next morning. That's about all I know. Now, Jabez, you can tell us something, I dessay.

---

*Lieutenant Thomas Fletcher Best joined the Navy as a 1st
class boy in 1808, and after serving in several ships as Midship-
man and Master's Mate, he joined the Revenue Cruiser Pigmy,
on the Weymouth Station, in 1817. While in her he pluckily rescued a boy from drowning by jumping overboard after him. From
1818 till 1821 he served as Chief Mate of the Drake Revenue Cutter, on the Plymouth Station; and while in her he crossed the
Channel in an open boat, and after lying off the Isle of Bas for
four days, succeeded in capturing a notorious smuggler. From
1824 to 1827 he served in the Hardy Revenue Cutter until pro-
moted to Lieutenant. From 1836 to 1839 he had command of the
Fox, after which he served in charge of a Coastguard Station on
shore. In 1822 he married a Miss Hicks, of Lanteglos parish.

J. S.—Aye, there's one or two things none of you has mentioned, which, may be, I can tell you about. I was living at Polperro time that affair came off, my father being chief boatman in the Coastguard there. I was at school then, may be about twelve year old. It was a Sunday morning, when a report came in that there had been fighting out at Lantic Bay, and that the smugglers had half killed some of the Coastguards. Of course, I went out along with a lot of other lads to see the fun, and when we got there we found the hedges broken down or with great gaps in them where the smugglers had forced through with their tubs. There was a tidy lot of people about, too. I joined the Fox soon after that affair, and when the men got yarning I used to hear a deal about it, and that is what happened. A cargo of tubs had been landed on the Friday night by the " Daniel and William," of Cossand, and put away in the cliff near the water. The party to run the tubs failed—perhaps made a mistake in the " spot "— and on Saturday morning the Fox passed on her way back from Plymouth, just about daylight, under charge of the gunner; the skipper being on leave. She scoured the coast as she went along, looking into all the bays to see if anything was on the move, or strange boats about, and the helmsman noticed a man on Pencarrow Point. Maybe it was Zebedee there looking after the sheep. Well, that same night—Sunday—after the Coastguards at Polruan had been mustered in the watchroom for duty, two of 'em— a commissioned boatman and an extryman—were sent along the coast to see if all was right. They got as far as Lantic Bay, where they sat down at top of the cliff, under shelter of a hedge, to have a pipe before turning homeward, and as they sat there yarning they heard a tramping of feet and voices, and presently a large party of men passed down on t'other side of the hedge, beating the bushes as they went, and saying to each other that the weather was too bad for any of the Coastguards to be out that night. " We shan't have any of them out here to-night "—those was the werry identical words they used. Well, directly Stevens twigged what was up he sent Varco, the extryman, back to Polruan to fetch out the rest of the crew. Presently he heard somebody whistling, and thinking it was one of the Coastguards, went to where the sound came from, and fell in with a party of smugglers, who set on him with bludgeons and drove him off. He fired his pistol, thinking to attract the Polperro men at the detachment up at Llansaloes, and then the rest of the smugglers gathered round him and told him they'd come to take the tubs away, and they defied the Coastguard to interfere with 'en. Stevens answered that the Fox's men would be out presently, and they'd see about that; upon which one of the smugglers swore at him, and said he'd seen the Fox going down to Falmouth, and she wouldn't be back that night. Well, the Fox went to Falmouth, sure enough, but she got back about ten o'clock, and was boarded by the Coastguard boat. And directly the Fox's men heard what was up they jumped into it, leaving only the boys on board, landed at Polruan, and hurried out as fast as ever their legs would carry 'em to Lantic Bay. When they got to what we used to call Lantic gate, just on the brow of the hill when you first get sight of the bay, the smugglers were on top of the hill opposite. I always understood they'd been delayed by the tide from getting down to the place where the tubs were stowed, or they would have had tubs and all away by that time. Anyway, they were making a terrible noise, swearing and shouting to the Coastguards, when Barrett, the riding officer, wanted to fire his pistol to let the coastguards know help was coming; but the others tried to dissuade him. However, he let off both his pistols, and, of course, the smugglers took alarm, threw down their tubs and bolted. The tubs were found afterwards lying all over the place—some had even rolled down into the bay. Some of the smugglers were caught, and if it hadn't been for that foolish fellow letting off his pistols a lot more would have been taken. Only one of the Coastguards was really hurt—Stevens, who stayed to watch the party; but I believe several of the smugglers were wounded, though they got clear off. The way the smugglers came to be acquitted up at Bodmin was like this. Their lawyer said they had no bludgeons with them, only common walking-sticks; but one of the Coastguards answered, "If you'd had one of them on your head you wouldn't have said it was a walking-stick!" Well, Magistrates and all were smugglers in those days, and so the jury gave the men the benefit of the doubt. Now, I believe that's the correct warsion of the run at Lantic Bay. Howsomesever, there's old Tom M., he was there, I reckon, let 'un give us his warsion of the affair.

T. M.—Yes, that's so, mate. But lor, my old brain box ain't what it waur; don't seem to work as it ought to; I've failed a goodish bit this year or two back; can't take my wittals like I did; no, nor my liquor, either, not but what, as you know, mate, I was a werry abstemious man at all times—never touched nothing stronger nor beer, unless 'twas a drop of Plymouth gin now and agin—at nights, you know, at nights. It's fine stuff for the kidneys, they say, taken last thing afore you go to bed hot, with a dash of ginger and leming in it. There was my old missus, now, she used to say——"

W. T.—Never mind the missus, old man; we want to hear what you can tell us of the affair at Lantic back along; you mind, don't ee?

T. M.—Aye, that I do! Why, didn't I nip one on 'em slipping through a hedge? I was a mariner aboard the Fox, time that affair came off. We left Plymouth the evening afore—if I don't mistake—and chased a wessel, in the morning watch, but lost sight of her in the haze. We allus believed it to have been the werry same vessel as landed the tubs the evening afore. From Fowey we ran down to Falmouth to fetch our rum, and left again that same afternoon for Fowey. Directly we brought up off Polruan the Coastguard galley came alongside and told us as how they'd discovered a party of smugglers at Lantic. I jumped into the boat with a lot more, and we hurried out. We could hear the smugglers shouting and kicking up a pretty shine while we was a mile off. When we was getting close up to them, one of the Coastguards sung out, "Come along, Fox's!" upon which a smuggler shouted back, with an oath, "D—— you, the Fox is gone to Falmouth!" The riding officer, Barrett, fired his pistol, and the smugglers made a rush to get away, chucking their tubs about all over the place. I grabbed one of the chaps as he was slipping through the hedge. He had a big stick in his hand, but he made no resistance after I got fair hold of him. Five more were taken, and their hands lashed behind their backs. They were put on trial for felony, as one of the Coastguards was hurt—you see the punishment for felony was a sight heavier than for smuggling; however, they were all acquitted. Thank'ee, Cap'n, I do feel a bit dry after all that palaver. Why, now, that do taste like the old stuff—is it Cherbourg or Rusco? Well, as I was just a-going to tell you, there was my old missus now, she used to say——"

EDITOR'S NOTE.

The affair at Lantic Bay was the last scrimmage of any importance between Coastguards and smugglers on the Cornish coast, and caused a good deal of excitement. Though, strange to say, the only allusion to it I have been able to discover in official records is a notation to the effect that, in October, 1835, " A reward was granted for a seizure made by the Polruan station and a detachment from the Fox cutter on the 29th March preceding; but no 'Head-money' was granted, none of the smugglers having been convicted."

It must be explained that the clause in the old Coastguard Instructions bearing on this ran as follows:—" Every person in the Coastguard is to consider it his first and most important duty to secure the person of the smuggler; and the reward of £20, granted for each smuggler convicted, will be paid to the person or persons by whom the smuggler is taken and secured."

In smuggling phraseology this " reward " was known as " blood money."

Richard Barrett, who commanded the party on this occasion, was the last of the old " riding officers " on this part of the coast. Beginning as merchant seaman, he joined the Revenue cutter service at the age of 15, in January, 1813, and the Coastguard in 1819. He resided at Fowey till the day of his death, in the seventies. His headstone may be seen in the cemetery.

At the time of the affair above described the coast to the eastward of Fowey was very imperfectly guarded, a circumstance of which the local traders were quick to take advantage. In consequence of this affray a watch-house was built at Lantivet Bay, and a detachment permanently located there, which effectually put a stop to the smuggling thereabouts. The cave in which the tubs were stowed is still in existence, close to high-water mark, in the cliff at Lantic Bay.

The " Daniel and William " herein referred to was one of the most famous smuggling vessels on the coast. Ostensibly a passenger boat, plying between Plymouth and Portsmouth, she contracted a habit of straying over to France, and was often seen at Roscoff—a circumstance which excited suspicions as to the orthodoxy of her proceedings. Her end was a tragic one.

MEETING THE SECOND.

Capt. S.—I have heard say them Fowey trawlers used to do a bit of quiet trading back along. Is that so?

W. T.—You'm right, old man. They carried on a pretty rig, right under the Coastguards' noses. Why, now, if you'll listen I'll pitch you a bit of a yarn about them trawlers—sly-boats, as they were. The game would never have been found out if it hadn't been for an informer; but, lor bless you, that's how it all came to be blowed on in time. Though I can tell you, the old Fox put a stopper on many of their games.

P. R.—Why, the old Fox was nothing better than a smuggler herself. I know that, for you see my niece married the mate, and I've seen the kitchen of the house where they lived hung all over with things brought from the Channel Islands—aye, and Cherbourg, too, what was contraband in them days; and I know for sartin sure he never paid a cent. of duty on them. Now that was a pretty game to carry on, and by them as was put there to stop smuggling! But 'twas always " set a thief to catch a thief."

W. T.—Fust of all, I must tell you I was sarvin' at the time as a mariner aboard the Fox, and there was a craft called the John as used to do a bit of trading between here and Plymouth. Sammy Sell, of Polruan, was cap'n of her—smart little chap he was, too. It was back in '38 I'm speaking of. You'll recomember old Sammy Sell?

P. R.—What, know old Sam! Why I knewed him as well as I knew my own brother! Didn't we wenture many a tub together?

W. T.—Well, old Sammy arranged with some parties round Fowey to fetch a cargo of tubs—300, I think—from Rusco, and run them in Fowey harbour. He got over to the French coast right enough, and just off Rusco fell in with the Susannah, a dandy-rigger cruiser, what belonged to the Cossand Coastguard station. She was a smuggler fust going off; had been captured by the Cawsand crew some years before, and then handed over to Mr. Foote, Chief Officer there, as a cruiser. She had tanned sails—same as she carried when a smuggler. Well, as soon as the John got near the Susannah some one on board the cruiser hailed and asked old Sammy where he was bound to, and Sammy, thinking she was a Cawsand smuggling boat, answered back, " Same place as you." Well, the Susannah didn't stop her, 'twouldn't have been any good, as she had no tubs in her then, and when Sammy got into Roscoff he found a lot more Cawsand boats there waiting for their cargoes; and the chaps aboard asked him if he had fallen in with any boats outside, and he said, " Oh, yes; we were hailed by a craft, and asked where we were bound," and when he described the craft, the Cawsand men said, " Why, that's the Susannah!" Well, old Sammy was that scared, he took nothing in but just sailed right back home again to Plymouth, and got safe in without even been boarded by the Coastguards. Sammy never went smuggling again after that. Then the smugglers chartered the Place, one of the Fowey trawlers, and she brought over 300 tubs and sank them off the Eddystone. The skipper said afterwards he was afraid to run into Fowey harbour with the goods, as he was deeper than usual, and the Coastguards would have suspected him. So, after sinking the tubs, he ran into Plymouth. Well, the owners began to suspect there was some game of this sort on, as the Place was away longer than usual, and I suppose they reported it to the Inspecting Commander, for we were sent out in the Fox to find her and bring her back to her owners so that she might get on with the fishing. We found her in Plymouth, and put one of our men aboard to bring her back—it was Richard Climo—and as they were running past the Eddystone a boy, who was on board, said quietly to Climo, " I know where there are a fine lot of tubs down!" So directly they got in to Fowey, Climo went aboard the Fox and told Cap'n Best what the boy had said. " Bring him on board," said Best. So the boy was brought aboard quietly so that none of the crew should know what was on, and he told all about the affair, and said the reason he informed was because the skipper of the Place treated him badly.   Cap'n Best ordered the Fox under weigh at once, and we took the boy along with us to show where the tubs were sunk.   Off Looe we ran into a calm, so both gigs were sent away to "creep" off the Eddystone.   I was in one, and we pulled straight away for the rock.   As soon as we got up to it the fog came on as thick as a hedge, and as the wind was puffing up wild-like, and it looked as if we were in for a dirty night, we got a hold of the lighthouse and hung on there, so that if it came on to blow we could climb aboard and save ourselves.   We lay there that night, and could hear the smugglers talking all round while they were trying to pick up their goods.   Of course, we could not tell who they were, no more than they knew that we were there.   The cutter didn't come up till late that night.   Next day we crept and crept pretty nigh all over the place without finding a tub, though we lost nine creepers amongst the rocks.   The boy said he was sure the tubs lay close to the light, as it shone right down on the deck when they were put overboard.   At last the boatswain said, " Well, there's only one spot we haven't tried yet, and that's under the bow of the Fox."   We put down the creeper and hooked up 45 tubs; what became of the rest I don't know, for we returned to Fowey after that.*

Capt. S.—Maybe you'll remember Dr. R——, of Fowey, back-a-long?   'Twas his father had the farm out by Llansaloes there.

J. H.—Ees; should think I did, old man, and a werry nice gen'leman he waur.   If a poor chap got hurt fetching a drop of sperrits up from the coast it was always "Let's send along for Dr. R——."   He was staunch, d'ye see, and knewed the walue of good sperrits as well as any man I ever com'd across.   I don't doubt but he larnt the trick from his old dad what used to wen-

---

*The official records contain the following significant entry :—
" August, 1837,—The ' PLACE,' ' ONE-AND-ALL," and ' BOCONNOC,' trawlers of Fowey, are strongly suspected of smuggling."

ture a tidy lot, 'specially about Chismis time, when ther was a
bit of jollification going forward. But, lor, times is changed, ye
don't get the same liquor nowadays. Ah! it waur a cruel shame
putting down that free-trading. I hear 'em talking a deal about
"free trade" now—"free trade," indeed, with 10s. a gallon on
sperrits and 5s. on a pound of cigars! Call that free trade?

Capt. S.—Never mind about that, let's hear what you can tell
us of Dr. R——.

J. H.—Well, the old doctor used to do a bit in the smuggling
line hissel. He was a wenturer, and was generally in partnership
with a farmer by name of P—— what had Lombart farm one time
—in Lanteglos parish—up by Mixtowe there.

P. R.—Him what was churchwarden, you mean? Aye, and a
good Christian man he was, too, and a regular churchgoer.

J. H.—That may be; but I'm now talking about his wenturing business, which he was pretty regular with too, I reckon.
Well, as I was saying, whenever the old doctor and his pardner
had business on they'd drive into St. Ossell together, to square up
accounts along wi' the smugglers, I suppose. Anyways, somehow or another, the doctor's share of the goods was always found
and seized by the Excise officer; no matter where he hid the stuff,
'twas sure to be sniffed out. That was a strange business now,
wasn't it? Of course, he couldn't make out how they always laid
their hands on it, though he suspected somebody had informed
agin him. Well, time went on, and one day when the doctor and
P—— had been in to St. Aus'll together, and they had finished
their business same as usual—'twas on a Friday, and they were just
agoing to start home—when P—— calls out, "hold on a minute,
I've forgotten something," and with that he runs back into the
house. Then it struck the old doctor, all of a sudden, that P——
'twas the party what had been informing on him all along; so,
without waiting another minute he druv home as fast as ever the
mare would take him—and it was a good mare he drove. And
directly he got back to his house he set to work and moved every
bit of stuff from where it was stowed into another place. Well,
sure enough, next day in comes the Excise officer, and goes

straight to the place where the goods had been laying fust going
off; but he found nothing. Dr. R—— asked him who it was
had informed agin him, but the officer said, "No, no; I can't
tell you that; but may be I'll give you a sign some day, and that'll
do as well!" And this was how he managed it. You must know
there was a public-house at Bodinnoc in them days, where a lot
of drinking used to go on of an evening amongst the farmers when
they met teogether. Well, one day when a lot of 'em was in there
drinking—P—— and Dr. R—— amongst them—in walks the Excise officer and claps down £50 in notes opposite to P——, and
says, "There you are, Jump, that's your share!" P—— started
up and said, "Jump! Jump! that's not my name!" Now, would
you believe it, he never put a finger on that money. The doctor
knew then who it was had informed agin him.

P. R.—Was his name Jump, then?

J. H.—Did ye niver hear why old P—— was called Jump? Then
I'll tell ye. He used to ride into St. Aus'll pretty often, and whenever he came back late at night, which was pretty often, too, and
found the ferry-boat tied up for the night, he'd swim his horse
across the river. Well, he came back one night with a drop too
much liquor in him—which wasn't an uncommon thing either—
and as it was too late for the ferry-boat, he put his horse into the
water as usual; but when he got out into the middle of the river
he found the tide too strong, and seeing he was being carried down
the harbour, he began to shout as loud as ever he could give
tongue, "One, two, three, jump! jump!" Well, they heard him
aboard the Fox cutter—aye, and 'twas lucky they did, or he'd
been drowned, sure 'nuff. I suppose old P—— thought he was
jumping a ditch. Anyway, the Fox put off a boat and picked
him up, and after that he was always called "Jump! Jump!"

Z. K.—P——, of Lombart, warn't the only one what went in
for that wenturing business; no, not by a long chalks. There was
a lot of farmers up Lanreath way did the same; aye, and many
of 'em ruined themselves by it. The one I was 'prenticed to, as
a lad, always had a keg hidden away up in a kind of hayloft.
The way I found it out was like this. One winter time, when

the other hands were off work, I and another shaver were sent to get hay from the loft, and while we were worriting about I spied a keg stowed away snug in a corner, so I says to myself, " I'll see what's in here," and with that I turned it up and had a regular good suck. It made me jolly drunk, for I wasn't used to sperrits. I had to go and drive the cows in. Well, I managed that, and then, thinks I, I'll take a bottle back and fill it up; but when I got back to the loft with my bottle and locked the door, taking the key along with me, I found all the stuff was gone. I felt pretty bad next day, and it was a goodish while before I had such another chance.

R. G.—Now we'm talking about smuggling, I can mind when two chaps—one belonging to Pelynt and t'other from Llansaloes —wentured a cargo, and handed over their money—a guinea a tub—to a man what was going over for the stuff. Well, the man took their money, but he never crossed, and they never saw either their money or the stuff. They were too much ashamed of being done to say anything about it; but I heard of it from one who knew.

Capt. S.—Well, times has changed a deal since those days. For my part I never knew any chaps who went in for that business do themselves good by it; 'deed, it was the ruin of most of them. There was P——, of Lombart; now he was sold up. Aye, and G——, who took the farm after him, he was broke. Then there was Dr. R——, he died quite poor. 'Twas all wrong, d'ye see?

Z. K.—Aye, and things has changed in other ways, too. Why, when I was a boy I was 'prenticed to a farmer at seven, and kept till I was 21; so there wasn't much time for larning Then look at the wages; they're much better all round now. Time I'm speaking of they was nine shillings a week, with corn, too, a deal dearer than it is now. I can tell ye everyone is much better off nowadays.

MEETING THE THIRD.

≋

W. T.—Since we met last I've been puzzling my old brain-box about that affair down to Coombe Horn what Tom was asking about. There was two runs thereabouts, if I mistake not; but the one I can mind was back in '44, when I was aboard the old Fox. She was laid up time I mean in Fowey Pill—where the station's to be, they say—under repair. It was in the afternoon, maybe about four o'clock, I had just landed at Polruan with the carpenter, when I see'd the Coastguard tearing down the rocks as fast as ever they could go, and into their galley. I thought something must be up, and, seeing the Chief Officer, Lieutenant Hooper, I asked him what it was. He said, "The Inspecting Commander is coming in the Eliza." But being a bit curious-like I stood and watched, and presently heard one of the men saying, "There's tubs to Coombe Horn!" With that I ran into the shed and told the carpenter—awful chap for swearing, he was; 'deed, I don't think he ever opened his mouth without cussing. Of course, he swore upon me, and told me I was a —— fool. I told him what the chaps was saying outside, but he only swore wuss. Howsomesever, I didn't mind, for he was 'spectable and sober, barrin' of his tongue, so I said to him again, "There's tubs to Coombe Horn." And I told him I'd heard the men talking about them. He began to think there must be something up then; but by this time the Coastguard galley had got well away, and was pulling like mad for the bay. Well, when we saw this we nipped down pretty smart into a boat, and we rowed arter them, and directly the boat touched the beach, alongside the Coastguard galley, we jumped out, ran the painter along the rocks, and nipped up to the hedge where Lieutenant Hooper was standing. All he said was, "You're too late, the seizure has been made;" and with that he told us to lend a hand and carry the tubs into the boat

and take them to the Custom house—the carpenter a-cussin' worse
than ever. Now, that seizure was made on information given to
the Riding Officer that very same afternoon. The smugglers were
believed to have been caught by the daylight coming on them
sooner than they expected, and so they hid the tubs in the "willy
garden" under the hedge.

R. G.—Reckon ye didn't make much out of that job, old man?

W. T.—Divil a penny. The other affair happened time I was
serving in the old Eliza—what was tender to the Polruan station.

J. S.—What; the craft that was sold out of the service some
time in the forties, and went a-smuggling?

W. T.—Aye, the werry same. Some of the Cossand chaps
took a run over to Rusco in her; but arter that she took to 'spectable trading. Well, you see, 'twas like this: one evening, winter
time, a Duloe chap came over to Fowey and told the Inspecting
Commander that a boat was expected in to land tubs at Bodinnoc, and that he had seen wagons waiting in the country to take
the tubs away. With that all the cutter's boats were ordered out
to row guard off the harbour mouth—the Coastguard being sent
along the coast. Piper, the man what was knocked about by the
smugglers, was down at Coombe Horn that night, and seeing a
boat come in took hold of the bow, when two men seized him,
took his pistols away, though not till he'd fired off one as an
alarm, and tied him down to the rocks while the tubs were run
and carried up amongst the elm trees near the farm. I allus
understood the craft what had the tubs in her was scared off the
harbour seeing so many boats about, and ran into Coombe Horn
as a quiet sort of spot. But there's Mr. S. there; maybe he can
tell you a bit more nor I can; 'twasn't much I see'd of the business.

J. S.—I ought to, for 'twas a night a man don't go to forget in
a hurry; 'deed, and an awfuller night I was niver out on, not a-
sittin' in a boat, leastways. Lord, I remember it well enough—I
was in the old Fox. It came about in this way. An Excise officer,
up to Lostwithiel, noticed two wans turn into the yard of a public-

house, and being a curious sort of a chap, he waited till the
driver had gone inside to get a bite and a sup and went and sniffed
around the wans. The fust one he looked into had two " creep
lines ;" that was enough for him, so he " pulled foot " into Fowey
as hard as ever he could go, gave information to the Inspecting
Commander, who ordered the Fox's boats outside to row guard.
The one I was in took station off the harbour mouth. It was a
ter'ble night—thunder and lightning, and rain in buckets—we had
to bale the boat out several times. While we laid under St. Catherine's Point, trying to get a bit of shelter, we saw a flash out
Coombe way and thought it was lightning. Next morning, about
daylight—we were out all that night, mind you—we saw a man
hurrying along the road over Point Neptune; he hailed us and
told us what had been done, and that there were tubs at Coombe
Horn. When we got round we found part of the tubs piled up,
and others floating about the bay. What had happened was this:
Piper had gone down into the bay, where a party of men, who
were waiting for the boat, seized him and tied him down, while
they ran the tubs. Some time after two of the Coastguards coming
along the cliff above whistled, and Piper called out to them;
meanwhile the smugglers had got clear. The boat that landed
the tubs was the Bodinnoc ferry boat; she had been taken from
her moorings and used to creep up with the tubs, and was laying
in Coombe Horn, swamped with the swell, when we got there. The
goods were believed to belong to parties about St. Germains, as
the vans had come from Plymouth. Now, I believe that's about
the rights of it. Eh, William! you was in the Fox then,
wasn't you?

W. T.—Yes; I guess you're about right. I believe two of the
Fox's men were along with Piper first going off. They all took
shelter in a cave out of the rain; and after a time Piper told
them he'd take a look round to the westward, and when he got
down to Little Coombe the boat was landing and he fired his
pistol afore he was seized. The Fox's men, being in the cave,
never heard the report, but two Coastguards did, and when they
found him he was lashed down, with the water pretty nigh up

to him. There was about seventy tubs taken. 'Twas the last run ever attempted on this coast, and the last bit of prize-money I ever got. There's Tom just come in ; he can pitch us a bit of a yarn about that affair down to Little Coombe—time old Piper was tied down. Cap'n wants to know the truth about it ; there's been a deal of nonsense talked of that affair.

T. M.—Why, now you come to mention it, I know what you mean. 'Twas back in '45, November month, I was a boatman stationed at Polkerris, where old dad was chief boatman. Lor bless you, it all comes back to me now just as if 'twas yesterday. Orders had come from the Inspecting Commander that afternoon to be ready for anything during the night, as a run was expected somewhere along the coast. Father and I were stationed at the Little Gribben—just inside the Big Gribben—towards Polkerris ; Lieutenant Hodge, the Chief Officer, and another man were down at Pridmouth, and one man was left at the station. It was a dark, drizzly night when we went out, and we were soon wet through ; but there was worse to follow. After we'd been out there sometime, father says, " Let's away down to Pridmouth, and see what's going forward there." Well, we were just starting off when I heard a shot. " Father," says I, " there's a shot !" " What are you talking about ?" he replied. I said again I'd heard a shot. " See what the time is," says he. I struck a match underneath my oilskin and looked at my watch—it was just two o'clock. we set off for Pridmouth, but there was no one about when we got to the bay. We thought it strange seeing no one there, and after staying till light began to break, we went home. When we got back we heard there had been something doing at Coombe Horn, and very soon knew all about the affair. I went in to Fowey next day and saw Piper. He'd been shamefully ill-treated —his arm was covered with bruises, and he was black and blue all over. He was on the sick list best part of a month. He told me he'd been standing along with a couple of men under a bit of shelter, looking out seawards, and after a bit he told them he'd go and have a look round the bay ; but the others said 'twas no good yet, as the tide was too low. However, he set off, and as he stepped on to the beach he was stoned, and as he stumbled the smugglers set on him with sticks, took his pistols away, and then tied him down close to the bow of the boat. Some of the Coastguards had been stationed inland, at the cross road, to intercept the goods in case they were run, and they found a wagon standing in a field, near the Menabilly Lodge, just off Coombe Lane. It had been taken in there to be out of sight. The Bodinnoc ferry-boat—the horse-boat—had been taken from its moorings the evening before, and carried outside the harbour with men hidden under the deck, and was used to creep up the tubs and land them. It was never found out who the goods belonged to, or who was concerned in the business down at the Coombe. The only clue we ever got was some years later from a woman down at Newtown, who said a man had come to her house that night, woke her up, and told her he had been badly cut across the forehead, and asked for something to put on it. They did say that Harris, one of the men that found Piper, fired his pistol at 'what he thought was a man making over the rocks, and the bullet may have grazed the man's forehead. It always seemed a rum thing how quietly that affair was managed, without anyone ever getting an inkling of the men who were down at Coombe that night!

Capt. S.—Well, ye see they had a good friend up at the farm yonder, above the Coombe. There was a tidy lot of stuff put away there without anyone ever being a bit the wiser.

T. M.—Old Tom B——, ye mean! He was a man of werry few words; but he was staunch. I allus understood there was a sly hole somewhere about the place; but 'twas niver found that I know of.

P. R.—Come in, Mr. Varco; werry glad to see you, though you bean't edzacly a regular member of this 'ere Society for the propagation of knowledge. We'm done a power of good already, and when the Cap'n there puts the Minutes into shape I don't doubt but what the Queen will want a copy. She was werry sweet on Fowey, they did say, and talked of having a willa built— a small place, not so grand as Buckingham Palace—where she could run down wi' the kids when there warn't much business going forward. She'd feel more homely-like than with all the swells and nobs hanging about her—the youngsters would be nice and safe in the Polruan ferry-boat along with Tom—he's used to the ways of the quality folk. Howsomesever, I 'spose we'm too old-fashioned here; though they tell me Mr. Hicks brings back a fine batch of smart Lunnon clothes when he goes up by 'scurtion from Par station wance't every two years. Oh, we'm moving ahead, and no mistake!

J. S.—If you want to see life ye mun go into Lostwithiel street of a Sunday night, when the chapel folk's coming out.

T. M.—Aye, there's a power of business doing in Fowey now. Why, I've seen a butcher's cart coming all the way from St. Blazey—there's sich a run on flesh-food now.

T. M.—Th' place ain't what it waur. Why, you know when my old missus——

P. R.—Oh, never mind the old woman; we'm here to improve our minds!

T. M.—I reckon though 't don't do to neglify the stomach; I'm a sort of dry.

P. R.—Why, old man, you'm had your 'lowance; we'm limited here.

Capt. S.—Well, Mr. Varco, we was just having a yarn about that affair time old Piper was tied down.

Mr. V.—What, at Coombe, d'ye mean, nigh fifty year back?
Capt. S.—That's it.

Mr. V.—Well, you've come to the right man; I can pitch you a yarn about that affair. I'd been out on business all day, away in the country, and as I expected to be late back I'd told my man to meet me at the Menabilly Lodge, by the cross roads. Well, it was very late when I got there, and I gave the usual signal, but there was no reply. Then I called out loud, " Joe!" and I heard a husky voice from the side of the road, " Ees, sur; havee seed mun?" " Seed who?" I said. " The smugglers; they be gone up—thirty 'osses—and I have had a good drink!" When I came to look for my man he was lying drunk in the ditch. Now, there's no doubt those were the very men who had been concerned in tying Piper down. That was about the last cargo ever run on this coast. I'm thinking, though, Joe must have seen double—me'be treble—with all the liquor he took aboard, for 'twas a wagon business that time, that's sartin sure.

Capt. S.—Well, Mister, now you'm found your way, maybe ye'll look in at our conversationes. I reckon you knows as much about the trade as any on 'em. There's one or two matters you can 'lighten us on, I don't doubt.

EDITOR'S NOTE.

Piper, the hero of the Coombe Bay episode, when describing his sensations, used to say that, before he was rescued, the water had reached to where he lay, and that he had given himself up for lost, the smugglers having tied him down to the " drift-line," to which the tubs were fastened.

The following extract from official records confirms the accuracy of the Society's Minutes :—

" Under date, Sep. 3rd, 1845, A General Order was issued to the Fowey Division of Coastguard to the effect, ' That an increased reward, to the extent of one-fourth : had been granted for the seizure made by part of the Polruan crew, at Coombe Horn, that Benjamin Harris and James Bain, boatmen of Polruan, had been noted for promotion when opportunity offered : and that the reward was to be distributed in the following proportions :—

	£	s.	d.
The Officer's legal share, ⅜th, amounting to -	56	6	5
To Excise Officer, as informer, ⅓rd - - -	18	15	6
For distribution according to C.G. Regulations -	37	10	11
To Jas. Piper, boatman, as remuneration for ill-treatment - - - - -	20	0	0
To Jas. Bain and Ben. Harris, £5 each, for assistance given - - - - -	10	0	0
For distribution according to C.G. Regulations -	56	6	5' "

The enterprising agriculturist who then occupied Coombe Farm was suspected of being connected with the smugglers. One who knew him well described him as "a very reserved man, who never seemed to speak out what was in his mind"—a trait of character which, doubtless, stood him in good stead in his relations with the free traders. Many years after his death some structural alterations at the farm disclosed the long-suspected "hide" or depot, consisting of a long, low, narrow cellar, running back into the country, to which access was obtained by removing the kitchen grate. This quaint relic of by-gone times no longer exists.

MEETING THE FOURTH.

J. H.—May be you can mind old Hockeday, him what had the Hall Farm back-along—me'be seventy year or more? Well, I can call to mind a queer thing happened to him once. He carried on a big butcher's business, and took his meat in to Polperro market, reg'ler, every week. I can see him now, sitting on the mare's rump behind his two paniers choke full of meat— that's the way he used to ride to market. We'm too proud to ride now, we must all hev a wheel-cart. But then you see the roads warn't up to much in they days. Arter he'd sold his meat he generally took back a couple of kegs of sperrits—if they was to be had reasonable cheap, which they was cheap, comparative, in them days—one keg in each pannier, nice and snug, like a couple of twins. Well, wanc't he was coming home—'twas evening, just about dusk—with a brace of tubs, when he heard a horse coming up behind, and saw 'twas the Supervisor of Excise. The kegs wasn't covered, and the old man could do nothing with 'em. " Good-night, Mr. Hockeday," says the Supervisor, as he rode past. " Good-night, sir," says he, thinking to himself, now I'm cotched, and no mistake. Well, he heard nothing more, but next market day, while he was standing at his stall, up comes Mister Supervisor. " Good-day, Mr. H——." Mr. H——, thinking something else was coming, began to talk of the weather and sich like, making hissel werry agreeable. At last he says, " Mr. Johns "—that was the Supervisor's name—" I'm just cutting out a nice steak for dinner, and shall be very pleased if you will join me." The Supervisor said he'd be werry pleased, and they sat down to a rattling good spread, with some fust-rate brandy grog afterwards. When it was time to be moving the Supervisor shook hands with Mr. H——, thanked him for the good dinner, and said to him, " Mr. H——, if I were you I'd cover up my mutton on the journey home!" I reckon old H—— took the hint.

P. R.—I allus heard the old man left a pot of money when he died.

J. H.—So he did; but may be you've heard tell that smuggling money did good to no one, and I reckon there ain't much of old H——'s money left now.

Capt. S.—Yess; and there was old Dr. R——, him we was talking about last confabulation—he drunk hissel into the grave, and some women folk, as ought to have knowed better, followed suit.

J. H.—Aye, and his old father, what had the farm out Polperro way, he made a lot of money, time and again; but 'twarn't no use. He was cotched, and exchequered for smuggling, and his farm broken up; and they said he died a werry poor man.

Capt. S.—Well, you see, 'twas like this: some on 'em had good luck, and some had bad; and I reckon we heard most of them what had bad luck.

W. T.—Aye, 'twarn't all plain sailing; no, not by long chalks —'twas a see-saw kind of life at best. There was my old dad, now —'spectable and sober—as knowed good liquor when he smelt it. He was druv to play the double-shuffle when times was hard and business slack. He was what they called a "spotsman" by trade —you'll know what that means, out and about the coasts all night, and all weather, spotting the places for the boats to come in with the goods, and flashing 'em off if the Coastguard was on the key-vivy, which wasn't werry often, else it would have been a poor sort of trade. Now, he earned his living, if ever a man did. When trade was slack the old chap was druv to find his bread somewheres in a 'spectable way, so he joined the King's sarvice, shipped aboard the old Fox, or the Harpee (Harpy), the wessel what was stationed down Plymouth way. When things brightened up agin he'd turn to his reg'lar trade once more. You see, in them days, a chap could leave the sarvice—prewentive sarvice afloat— with 28 days' notice; so as soon as old dad seed things brightenin' up he'd hand in his warning and be off. Sartinly, he sometimes lost the fust of the flood; but he was a rare hand at making up

leeway. He was three times aboard the old Fox, and left the sarvice at last with a pension of £39 " per hannum," as he used to say
when he was axed about his pension. He was such a waluable
man they couldn't get on without him at last, so he shipped out-
and-out, quite 'spectable and reg'lar. I will say this, he never
made no pile of prize-money, for he was an honest a man as ever
lived, and would have scorned to rob a poor smuggler of his goods.
'Twas the old man's boast, to the day of his death, that he could
say, along with old Admiral Benbow, " What little I've got, I've
got honest; it never cost a seaman a tear, or my country a far-
thing."

Capt. S.—Ah, 'tis a grand thing to die with a clean conscience!

T. M.—Yess; times has changed! There was my old missus
now——

J. H.—All right, old man, we've heard about the missus before. We'm here for novelties; ain't that so, Cap'n? Maybe some
of you will mind old Pascoe? what lived out Menabilly way—a
nice 'ospitable fellow he was, always glad to see a chap drop in—
he had about the best brandy round about—you'll know how he
got it, but that ain't no business of mine. Well, one morning his
shepherd was out on the cliffs, by the Gribbon, looking arter the
sheep, and he spied a flock down on the beach, but they wasn't
sheep, though they'd got strayed somehows—tubs they was, sixty
on 'em, broken away from the sinking line, I 'spose. He warn't
long reporting the find to the master, and before the Coastguard
came sniffing along, as they mostly used to, at daylight, the
wagons was down and the flock safely stowed in a private pen up
at the farm. Well, after a time, Mr. P—— came in for a bit of
a fortune and retired from his farm; went away west, by Penzance, to settle down for the rest of his days. All his 'longings was
carried away in carts, and amongst the lot was two hogsheads of
cider—leastways they called it cider—but for matter of that
'twas best French brandy what never paid a ha'porth of duty—all
carried in open day for fifty miles through the country, and no
one a bit the wiser. 'Twas a fine stock; but whether it lasted
him out I can't go for to say.

Capt. S.—You'm alright, as far as you've got; but I reckon you've left out the best of the pudden. Afore Mr. P—— got his 'longings clear he had word the Coastguard was coming up to search, so he hurried up with his cider casks, and had 'un in the cart ready for a start by the time the prewentive-men came along. "What's all this?" said the officer. "Oh, I'm just sending off some cider; will ye have a drop?" Well, no one ever knew a prewentive-men refuse a drink, and being a bit sweaty, with the walk up, they said they'd be werry glad. "Well," says Mr. P——, "you'd best come inside and sit down while the girl draws off a jug, for I reckon the stuff in they casks ain't fit for the likes of you, being all shaken up with the worriting about." So they sat down and got chatting quite 'greeble-like, and had a nice glass of bright cider afore they 'gan to sniff around. By the time they was ready for work, d——d if the cart hadn't druv off; and, would ye believe it, they pudden-headed prewentive chaps was niver a bit the wiser for what had been going on under their werry noses!

J. H.—Mr. P—— was werry friendly with the orficer at Pol-kerris; 'twas a bit quiet down there, so the orficer used to go up and spend the evening along with him. I don't mean to say there was any collision between them, but they'd meet together like gentlemen, and 'twouldn't have been good manners to go for to ask where the liquor came from, though anyone might guess by the flavour of it.

R. C.—You was talking about the stock he took away with him. Well, I knew the old chap as well as anyone, and arter he got settled into his new house—a nice little place, too, werry pretty, and all that—arter he got settled down I went to see him. He'd married a real lady, and wanted for nothing; but it was easy to see what lay they was on—the brandy was into their faces, and afore many years was out they'd drunk themselves to death.

Capt. S.—Now you come to mention that sort of finish, there was him what was keeper at Menabilly. Oh, 'twas seventy year agone; he had as good an eye for twigging tubs on the beach as ever he had for birds! Aye, many is the tub he picked up, and

D

carried home. Well, he had a soaking sort of an end. They did say 'twarn't safe to go nigh him with a naked light—he was full of what they call " Spontanibus combustible."

J. H.—Aye ; I've heard say it was a dreful sort of death. They gets red hot through like a heap of clinkers, and then busts all to pieces, though I never seed such a one mysel ; no, and don't want to this side of the grave. I 'spose 'tis a sort of judgment on 'em for wastin' liquor.

Z. K.—'Tis surprising how tricksy some folks get when they're like to lose their liquor. There was old W——, lived out Polkerris way ; he'd just got his keg of sperrits for a Chrismis store, but somehow the Coastguards sniffed it out, and came up to search. Well, the old chap spied 'em coming along from the kitchen window, and what does he do? Why, he claps the stuff into the kettle, and puts it aside of the fire ; and when the prewentives come in they never thought of putting their nose into the kettle, so the old man saved his Chrismis supply. 'Twas a kind of tricksy, now, warn't it?

J. H.—'Tis strange how things come back to one when people gets talking. I can mind now, back along, me'be sixty year ago, there was a Collector of Customs at Fowey who was werry fond of a drop of sperrits, when they was to be had cheap. He was an upright man ; did his duty strict and without favour, but there was one thing he niver could stand, and that was wanton waste—it regular shocked him, and he warn't a nervous man neither, so to speak. Well, I must tell you there'd been a seizure of tubs down the coast—everything was brought to Fowey Custom House then, and for some cause or other orders had come down from headquarters to start the liquor into the harbour. 'Twas a scand'lus command, but a horder is a horder, and the Collector, being a Christian gemmon, and as honest a man as ever stepped, saw there was nothing for it but to do as he was bid. So with that he ups with the tubs and sets the liquor a-flowing into the sea like. But being an inwentive sort of chap, with a werry proper horror of waste, he rigged up a kind of a gutter-thing under the wall where the sperrits was to be started, running away into a sort of cellar place, where, as chance would have it, there was some empty casks with their bungs out. Well, somehows the liquor ran into this 'ere gutter-thing, and a chap what happened to be in the cellar place, seeing the brandy running along and likely to run to waste and flood the place, what did he do but points the end of the gutter-thing over one of the bung holes and saved the mess. Well, now would you believe it, all that there brandy ran away into them there casks in the cellar. Now, that was a tricksy thing, if you like! What became of it arter I niver heard, and shouldn't like to say for sartin; but if I'd been Collector of Customs, in his place, I know what I should have done with the stuff.

P. R.—Aye, 'twas a Christian act, and no mistake. 'Deed, I'm thinking when he came nigh his end he might console hissel with the refraction that he'd done the State some service by saving it from the scandal of sich a thing as was ordered.

Mr. V.—Now, I 'spose there ain't many here as can remember the time when there was no Coastguard—nothing but Riding Officers and a party of Drag-goons what stayed up to St. Ossel— that was more nor seventy year agone. I lived up at Tywardreath then, and seed some funny games. I don't suppose you could name anyone then what didn't smuggle, or, leastways, what didn't drink smuggled sperrits, when they was to be had. There was my old dad, now—a good man, he was—honest and sober, what niver cheated the country of a ha'penny, he allus bottled off his sperrits as soon as he got them—'twarn't safe to leave the stuff lying about in tubs—and arter they was bottled off the bottles were put away on a shelf in a cupboard. Well, one evening we was all seated quiet when bang—there was a scranch of broken glass in the cupboard, and a stink of liquor fit to knock you down. 'Twas the shelf had given way, and the brandy was running all over the floor and out of the door. Oh! mussy on us, it was cruel to see all that good brandy wasting, for it niver stopped till it got into the street. "Well," says mother, after it was all gone, "'tain't no good crying over spilt milk, even it 'tis brandy." Talking about smuggling, why, they don't know what

it means nowadays. I can remember, in times back, seeing forty
or fifty horsemen riding through Tywardreath of an evening, each
carrying a couple of tubs slung across the saddle. Aye, and a
jolly lot of chaps they were, too. They halted in the village,
spiled a couple of tubs and let anybody who liked come · ɪd
have a suck at the spile-hole; and you may be sure chaps warn't
backward. The goods had been landed at Polkerris—a nice
quiet spot then. Ah! it do make one a bit tearful to think of
them times, and good, pure sperrits within the reach of every poor
man.

J. H.—Aye, 'twas werry well so long as there warn't no fighting; but at times, when the Excise orficer was an onrasonable
man and hard on the poor, there was cruel work. There was a
set-to wans't at a farm up by Lanreath. 'Twas afore my time, but
I've often heard the old folks talking about it. It seems the
Riding Officer and some of his men came up with a party of
chaps carrying tubs, and told them to give up their goods. That
was a likely thing, warn't it? Well, of course, they refused and
began to show fight, when the prewentive men tried to get hold
of the tubs. One of the smugglers—I don't remember his name
—was shot in the breast; he fell flat on his face, but jumped up,
and after shouting to the rest, "We'll win yet," dropped dead.
He was a waliant sort of a chap, you see. There had been an
informer, and that was how the prewentive men came on the
party. When the brother of the poor chap who had been shot
found this out, he was ter'ble wild, for you see his brother had
lost his life through it.

J. A.—You'm right; there was some tidy battles* back-
along, and 'twarn't only the men what fought; some of the women
did a bit in that line, too. There was old Susan Light, now;
she'd sit and yarn by the hour about all the battles she'd had
with the Excise-men. 'Ess, that's so. Lord, I remember her
well—a great strapping woman she was. She had a fair stand-

---

*An old man, who had been Sexton at the Parish Church in
former days, died at Polruan during the seventies, with a bullet
ensconced in his arm, which he had received in a severe fight with
the Coastguard, between Polperro and Looe, in 1831.

up fight along with an Excise-man—aye, and knocked him down just as any man would. You'll remember her, Tom, no doubt? —a tremenjious, great, long, straight woman—she'd keep the chaps laughing by the hour, with her way of telling things. There ain't none like her now, I reckon! Well, after she'd knocked that fellow down—mind you, it was a regular fight and fair play business—the Excise-man said he would let them take their goods away, if so be as they would tell him who the man was—he made sure it was a man, you see; he never would believe it was a woman knocked him down. Poor old Susan! her's bin dead a brave while now, and I reckon there's werry few remembers her.

J. H.—Oh, aye; there was some desperate battles at times along with the Excise-men inland—that was when they wouldn't come to an agreement like reasonable folk. Now I comes to think on it, I can call to mind one affair werry well, for I knew the man what saved the Excise-man's life, and he told me how it all came about—Francis Couthe was the man's name. 'Twas like this: the smugglers came across the Excise-man from Caw-sand—a busy man, he was. Well, he wanted to take their tubs, so there was a bit of a flare up, and the smugglers knocked him down and were like to have killed him, not being over merciful when they were carrying tubs. It was beat, beat, beat with their sticks until the poor chap could hardly speak. Then Couthe, seeing there was going to be murder, laid himself across the man, and told 'em they'd be killing him too if they didn't stop their beating. Well, he saved that Excise-man's life, though, to be sure, he got a ter'ble blow on the side from one of their sticks; but he knew well enough that if the Excise-man was murdered someone would blow the gaff, and then they'd all hang for it. That Excise-man was a game fellow, too; for after he'd picked hissel up he challenged any one of 'em to fight. Oh, I've heard Couthe say many a time, that if it hadn't been for him getting between the man and the sticks, they'd have killed him sure enough. He said they were a passul of d——d scamps to use a man so. Couthe met the man many years after, and when they got yarning over the affair, he told him how he had saved his life; and, what's more, he carried the mark of it on his left side to the grave with him.

MEETING THE FIFTH.

ADDITIONAL MEMBERS OF THE SOCIETY.

Jacob C.   ... An old Revenue Cutter's man.
William L.   ... Formerly a Protector of the Revenue.
Richard H.   ... A merchant from the Eastward.
William H.   ... An old smuggler, whose name often appears
                           in official records.
Richard J.   ... An old Revenue Cutter's man.

Capt. S.—You've been knocking about these parts a goodish while, John—do'ee remember a chap called Kingcup—Richard was his name, I think.

J. C.—What! Dickey Kingcup? Why, bless thee, I knewed him as well as my own brother. Now, he waur a proper smuggler, he waur, and no mistake; a reg'lar out-an-outer, I may say. Know Kingcup, indeed! Why, there wasn't a keener smuggler on the coast. I saw a deal of him when I lived at Fowey, back-along. Dickey was in the Coastguard then. Why, now, that must have been back in 1825, or thereabouts; anyhow, it waur a brave while back, and no mistake. Yes, he was a prewentive-man then; but, lor bless you, he spent the chiefest part of his time at the Ship Inn—if you wanted him you'd be sure to find him there. He never went out at night, patter-rolling along the coast, I mean, and I don't believe he would for any person whatever.

Capt. S.—You'm right, old man; he used to be werry thick with the smugglers while he was here, but he was pretty closely watched. You see, the officer smelt a rat, and that's the reason Dickey had to clear out at last. Now, he was a sly one, if you like—a sharp fellow, too. Oh, I can mind him well enough!

W. L.—Now you mention his name, I can tell 'e something

about old Dickey. He was too sharp for the Coastguard, and as he couldn't get his promotion he chucked it, and set up a public-house on the quay here, called the " Crown and Anchor;" aye, and a werry comfortable house it was—he knew where to get good sperrits, you see! He took to smuggling reg'lar then; a proper busy fellow he was. I've been sent down to watch him myself at Bodinnoc. Arter a bit he went to live at Plymouth; but he was often round about Fowey on business. Whenever he turned up it was, " Look out sharp, Kingcup's about again!" He set up as a shipbroker at Plymouth, and made believe he came down here to look after ships; but we knew well enough what his game was, and two or three of us were always told off to report his movements. They did say he had a brother an Admiral.

R. J.—That's so, old man. I knew all his family well—they belonged down Yealm way—'deed, I may say, we was all play-mates together when we was young. Dickey—that's the one who was in the prewentive sarvice—was one of the most notorious smugglers on the coast. There's no knowing how many tubs he ran up Fowey Harbour—many hundreds, if the truth be known. He led the Coastguard chaps a pretty rig; you see he knew all their routine, from having been in the service. He was a deal about Fowey—there was always a cargo expected about Christ-mas time. I lost sight of him arter he settled at Plymouth; but I know he was knocking about on this coast for a brave while arter he'd sarved his 'prenticeship in the Coastguard. Dickey warn't sharp enough, once though, for he was taken down on Lantivet beach waiting along of a party of men for a boat to come in. 'Twas my father took him. He went up to Dickey, tapped him on the shoulder, and said, " I arrest you in the Queen's name." Dickey replied, " Well, Mr. Jenkins, you'm the only man I'd allow to arrest me!" I don't know what was done to him, but as there were no goods took, I 'spose he got clear; he was a smart little chap. But there's Will H—— coming in, he'll be able to spin you a yarn about Dickey Kingcup, for he worked along with him, hand and glove. Eh, Bill?

W. H.—You're right, old man; there's no one here knowed
him better. He and I worked together for a brave while, and
did a lot of business; 'deed, we was just like brothers while we
were in co'. He was a nice fellow, too. You might always
know him, because he would wear gilt buttons on his coat,
like an officer. He was in your sarvice, John, once; but he got
mixed up along with the smugglers and had to clear out, that's
about the long and short of it—he was hunting with the hounds
and running with the hare, and someone informed agin him, and
so, of course, he was obliged to go. For all that he was a smart
chap, and a clever one; 'deed, he was up to every dodge, and he
knew all about the Coastguard routine, as well he might, though
I never listened much to what he said—it was just mind no one's
tale in those days, but take care of yoursel. You see, chaps
might be pretending to tell you some secret, and all the time
they'd be letting you in. No; 'twas always safest to keep your
own counsel. How I came to know Kingcup was like this.
Arter he left the Coastguard he set up a beershop on the quay
here, and as I was pretty often in Fowey on business we used
to meet—birds of a feather, don't you see. He was a spirited
man; but the worst of him was he would get drinking and then
he'd get to chaffing, and that wasn't the way to do business. Now,
this'll show you the sort of chap he was. Maybe you'll know the
public-house you pass coming up on to the moor from Looe, on
the road to Lanreath? It used to be called "The Hatchet"—we
called it "The Axe," for you see the sign was an Axe. Me'be
it's all gone now—I'm speaking of forty or fifty years back.
Well, one night Kingcup and I were taking a wagon load of tubs
along there—the goods had been landed at Looe—and we pulled
up at "The Hatchet" to get a drink. But Dickey Kingcup was
half-seas over already, and he began shouting for liquor, and
when it was brought him it wasn't to his liking, so he chucked
it on the ground, glass and all. Oh, a tidy shindy he made, I
can tell you! But that was his way when he had liquor in him.
We crossed over together more than once. One time I wentured
£20, and he put in £50. We sunk that lot off Portscatho Beach.

Oh, he must have made a good thing by it in his time; for you see he set up arterwards at Plymouth as a shipbroker, and was in co.' with Kirken and Couch and the rest of that lot; and he'd talk with the captains and arrange with 'em about fetching over goods; that's what took him about so much along the coast; and, likely enough, he'd wenture some pounds hissel. And then, being in with the gentry, he could allus get together as much money as he wanted for a cargo. The first business I and Kingcup were in co.' together over was down the coast by Carhayes, where we ran a lot of cargoes on Port Luny Beach. We bought an old galley that had been a prewentive boat, and called her the Happy-go-Lucky, and kept her down there till we'd finished the job. She was taken arterwards, at Falmouth, on suspicion, and cut up; but she was pretty well worn out then. The first time I crossed with Dickey was in the Arethusa, of Cawsand—as smart a little craft as ever sailed—about 20 ton, dandy-rigged, painted black, with tanned sails. Coming back, we had to sink the goods off the Dodman. It's a queer spot off there, as you know, Cap'n. In some parts there's mountainous rock standing straight up from the bottom—them's the places where the Gorran men put down their pots—and then, all of a sudden, it runs off to deep water. We took soundings afore we put the goods down, and got twelve fathoms, which we thought would be a nice depth of water; but we sunk 'em much closer in shore than we took it to be at night; consekintly, when we began to lift the tubs, we found the bottom ran off to a great depth, and the best part of the crop had gone over the rocks. We only saved forty out of 108 we brought across—'twas a fool's job. The reason we put them down there was that we might get the Gorran crabbers to work the goods when they were lifting their pots. It took a werry good glass, aye, and sharp sight, to make out what a man was doing at that distance from the shore—whether he was lifting pots or tubs. The crabbers would raise a few tubs at a time, and bring them ashore underneath their pots. There was a power of stuff landed like that. Forty tubs was all we raised out of that lot; you see, we had to cut the drift-line. Oh, it was a darned clumsy job!

W. T.—You'm left out one thing, Bill—time Dickey King-cup was took down at Par. Reckon I was at the taking of him. I was stationed at Polkerris 'long with my father, who was chief boatman there, back in the forties, I reckon. 'Twas morning time; I was watchman, and seeing a new wessel—a schooner—going into Par Bay, I boarded her. She'd no licence nor number. Looking round, I see'd a man in the cabin. "Hullo, cap'n," says I, "who's this?" "Oh, it's a man I brought round from Ply-mouth." Looking in I recognised Kingcup; course we all knew him well enough—we'd reason to. "Oh, Mr. Kingcup, is that you?" says I. "Oh, my!" said he, "this is a bad job." I went back for father and the officer—Mr. Hodge—and they boarded the wessel, and took her round to Fowey. What happened to Dickey Kingcup I can't say; but I remember getting some money for the job—there was something wrong with the wessel. I reckon though we shouldn't 'a been sorry to see him locked up, for he gave us more bother than anyone else on the coast.

R. J.—Oh, aye, he was a smart chap, and no mistake. The Kingcups were relations of ours. The Admiral—that was Dickey's brother—and my mother were werry great friends—brought up together as children; 'deed, he was werry fond of her—called her Becky, and allus used to come and see her when he was home from his voyages. There was another brother—Phil, I think—who was a great smuggler, too; but I don't rightly mind what became of him.

W. H.—He was wrecked in a Cossand boat off the Mew-stone; his head was found arterwards in the cuddy of the wessel. There was three other men from Yealm along with him, poor chap. But there, they wern't the only ones what lost their lives over that business by a long chalks. Ah! 'twas bitter work of a winter time—that crossing from Rusco and Cherbourg—sleet and snow, and blow, blow, blow, fit to tear your hair off. By gosh, if I was to tell the young chaps nowadays what I've been through they wouldn't believe me. They seem a different breed, to my mind, to the chaps of sixty or seventy year back; they ain't got the go in 'em for that smuggling business, not now; they'm all too 'spectable, I 'spose.

R. H.—That's true what you say about poor Phil Kingcup being lost. I was coming back from Cherbourg the same night; werry stormy, it was, though I've seen it wuss, still there was the douce of a kick-up of sea. We was going to start together; but when we got under weigh Phil sung out they wouldn't be ready for another half-hour—had to get their to'sl down and stowed. However, after a bit, we see'd 'em following, and that was the last was ever seen of the boat under sail. Next that was heard of her was when she drifted on shore, with all her tubs hung round her, and the ballast gone, by Hope Cove. The bodies—four of 'em—was seen lying on the bottom, in deep water, just outside. I saw them mysel; 'twas the strangest sight I ever see'd, for you could tell their faces as they laid on the bottom, it was that clear. That was the end of poor Phil Kingcup. What became of Dickey I don't know.

W. H.—Why, now, I can tell you. He caught cold at election time and died—me'be thirty or forty year ago. Aye, he was a smart little chap, and no mistake; and I don't doubt but what he made a pile.

EDITOR'S NOTE.

From official documents we learn that the "notorious smuggler," Richard Kingcup, joined the Coastguard in 1824; served at the Polruan station as commissioned boatman till 1828, when, having discovered his true vocation, he withdrew from the Government service, set up as a publican at Fowey, and came to be regarded henceforth as a professional smuggler; though, strange to say, he figures in official documents, as late as 1830, as "Surety for the mate of the Revenue cutter Fox," to the amount of £200.

From the records of the Preventive service some further items of information concerning the activities of Mr. Richard K—— during the next twenty years have been gleaned, as follows:—

1833.—Was seen at Plymouth the same day as the "Good Intent," of Portsmouth, arrived, after sinking her cargo.

October.—R. K., of Fowey, is believed to be mixed up with the "Tam-o'-Shanter," of Fowey.

November.—Has been seen moving about in a suspicious manner in company with Abrm. A——, of Downderry, and Hicks, of Fowey. Is supposed to be arranging a cargo.

1834, February.—Is believed to be concerned in the open boat "Unity," which is bringing over 200 tubs.

Was seen at St. Stephen's, and is believed to be connected with a cargo to be run up the Truro river by Ellory of Probus.

Was seen on the move with his party in connection with the "Bee," "Dove," "Four Brothers," and "Good Intent," all of Cawsand.

April.—Is supposed to be connected with the "Harmony," in co. with George Kirkin.

May.—Arranging for a cargo to be brought over by a French vessel, in co. with Kirkin, Hambly, and other Plymouth smugglers.

July.—Believed to be connected with the "Liberty," trawler, of Plymouth, and to have been across in her.

Reported to have hired the open boat, "Four Brothers," to bring over a cargo for the Fowey district, as he has been absent from Fowey several days.

September.—Was seen at Plymouth the same evening as the "Providence and Anne" sailed on a smuggling trip.

October.—Is seen at Plymouth, and reported to have engaged a Fowey sloop.

November.—Seen at Plymouth conversing with the master of the "Daniel and William," and then set off for Looe.

December.—Seen at Plymouth talking with the master of the "Experiment," trawler, and is reported to have run a cargo in Falmouth harbour.

Was at Plymouth in co. with a Lostwithiel man engaged in smuggling.

1835, January.—Is believed to be concerned with Thompson, of Lostwithiel, in the "Hope," of Devonport, seized in Yealm river with 317 tubs and 13 flagons concealed under dung.

July.—Seen on board the "Jane," of Fowey. Is said to have a brother serving on board the Fox R.C. at Fowey.

1837, November.—Has sunk a cargo in St. Austell Bay. Will employ the Cawsand galleys to work it.

1838, May.—Has bought the schooner, "Henriette," in co. with Kirkin, for smuggling; she is 60 tons—was formerly of Scilly.

1840, September.—Was on board the trawler, "Two Brothers," of Plymouth, when seized by the Tide Surveyor there with 31 cwt. of tobacco, no doubt taken out of the "Good Intent." Old Cudlip was on board.

1842, July 1st.—Was seen near Fowey, on the road to Charlestown.

July 18th.—Returned to Fowey; is still hanging about, and is believed to be concerned in the "Le Oif," French smuggling cutter.

1844, February.—Landed at Polkerris. A sharp look-out to be kept on his movements.

July.—R. K——, the "noted smuggler and broker of Plymouth," is reported to have gone west.

1848, July.—Is somewhere in the Fowey district. To be strictly watched.

1850, June.—Seen at St. Austell in co. with George Kirkin.

April.—At Pentuan, near Mevagisey, in constant communication with the master of the "Secret," of Poole, late a Revenue cutter.

MEETING THE SIXTH.

~~~~~~

P. R.—Well, Cap'n, seems to me we've a-gotten together a wast of information about the trade. I reckon by the time Mister there gets it shaped up a bit and put tidy, 't'll make a grand volume—what they calls a Cyclopeedy. 'Twill make a nice 'ittle keepsake for Her Majesty, just for old time's sake—something to read of a Sunday afternoon arter dinner. I tell ee, though, I've been revoluting the matter over in my brain-box since last meeting, and I'm thinking we've a left something out. We've never had no proper confabulation about whether the trade was good or bad for the country; not that there's any question about it to my ways of thinking; but there's folk as says twarn't a 'spectable way of arning a living, as if the goods wasn't paid for afore they left the merchant's, and sold, all fair and above board here. To my mind, competition ain't a bad thing, and if we could sell the stuff a bit cheaper than the dooty-paid, where's the harm? Live and let live's my motto, and darn the Government.

J. A.—You'm right, old man; them's my sentiments to a T; but we'm old-fashioned, they say.

Capt. S.—Ees, me'be we'm a bit behind the times in thicky parts. But 'twas that there Wesley guv the trade a bad name to begin with; aye, and ever since he came 'postulating down west there's been folk who niver set eyes on a tub of sperrits, but who'd hang every poor chap what had a hand in the business—the good with the bad—the honest, 'spectable traders what never watered the sperrits, along with drinking blackguards as cheated every wenturer what trusted 'em with money; they'd a-hung the lot, if they'd had a say in the matter.

Z. K.—Say, old man, it's allus been a wonder to me that Wesley ever got back out of the Duchy with the skin on his back.

They was werry long-suffering, surely, to let a man like that go on preaching agin their manner of earning a living. Ees, 'twas wonder they chaps down west—a rough lot they was, by golly— 'twas a wonder they didn't cut 'en up and put 'en in their crab pots, same as they sarved Job Ockady, up on the north side yon- der—that there 'Ciseman what got shoving his nose into other folks' business.

Capt. S.—He waur a grand talker, and I reckon he talked 'en over; but I do think he waur a bit prejudiced—setting his face agin the trade like that. No doubt that's why the Church folk turned agin him. There's good and bad sperrits, same as there's good and bad angels, so we'em told, though I ain't never run agin they feathered folk mysel, and to preach down sperrits of all sorts was foolish like, to my ways of thinking. There's no doubt he turned a power of people agin the trade. But what was pore chaps to do as couldn't afford the price of the dooty-paid? Sure 'nuff there was English gin, but you couldn't put that along- side French brandy; no, nor Hollands, though to be sure there was some as said they was too heating, 'specially for the women- folk. Well, the sperrits being dear 'twas a werry good thing for the country that them as couldn't pay for the dooty-paid should have a chance to get a sup now and agin at a reasonable price. Ain't that right? Why to be sure!* And then, look what a 'spect- able calling it was back-along. Why, there warn't a gintelman fore and aft the county but had a hand in the trade. I don't go for to say that the Lord Liftennant ever wentured a tub—no, nor the Dukes of the Duchy—they had to keep same side as the Government, knowing which way their bread was buttered;

---

*Capt. Stockhollum was by no means singular in his views. In the year 1800 the Royal Courts of Guernsey, in their reply to expostulations from the British Government about smuggling from the Channel Islands, pleaded that "The spirits which are brought here and sold to the smugglers are all low Hollonds proof. . . . . If we are rightly informed, what is smuggled from this island, or Roscoff, is generally sent to Cornwall or Devonshire, and mostly disposed of to some thousands of miners of those counties, who mostly live underground, to whom spirits are beneficial, but who, nevertheless, could not afford to pay for entered spirits."

me'be, too, they couldn't take sperrits—they quality folks drinks
nowt but sour wines, clairit and sich like, so I'm told. But what
I mean to say is, that there was werry few of the quality that
didn't buy the stuff when it was sold to 'em; aye, and preferred
it to the dooty-paid sperrits.

P. R.—Thicky's gospel truth. Why, now, ye'll mind old
Squire Tregaminion, what lived at Carhayes back-along? A
werry nice gen'lman he waur, and kind to the poor, and a werry
good friend to them as carried on the trade at the risk of their
lives. He allus kept his park gates open so that they could come
through with goods arter dark, when the land sharks was patter-
rolling the main road with their darned cutlashes and pisterolls,
like a passul o' highway robbers as they were. Well, now, I can
tell ye summut ye've never heard tell of before, me'be. Sum on ye
will be able to mind the young Squire—the eldest son, I mean—
a larky young fellow he waur, and no mistake. Well, he was
allus badgering Tom Hicks, the blacksmith up on the hill, to
get money collected for a cargo and cross over with him. "Na-o.
na-o," old Tom used to say, "The Squire 'll be tarnin' me out
of the place if he hears of it." But young Mister Dick he kept on
at him and guv him no peace of mind till he consented. Well,
the long and short o' the matter was Tom got some parties to wenture—young Mister put in something, too, I reckon—and they
crossed to Rusco, got their goods, and ran 'em up the Truro river.
Now, that's gospel truth. Aye, and when the old Squire heard
of it he nigh split his sides with laffin'. Ah, the old Squire was
a kind man to the pore.

J. H.—Aye, and th' passons was werry different back-along
to what they is now; reckon they knew the wally o' pure sperrits,
and warn't too grand to buy them from the pore chaps what risked
their lives to keep the parish supplied. 'Twas soverin' remedy in
collic and brown typhus, when doctors warn't so common in the
land, and med'cins was dear for poor folk. The churches, too,
was handy places for putting tubs into, 'til sich time as the wenturers could fetch 'em, 'specially when there was waultses; that's
where they had the pull of the chapel folk. Aye, and I don't doubt

but that's what made Wesley so down on the trade. Lord, what a pretty lot of tubs I've see'd passed into church of a Saturday night! I don't 'spose there's a church anywhere nigh the shore in the Duchy but what's had a crop of goods laid in it. Th' passons didn't mind—of course they was paid their tithes all fair and above board. Aye, and there's been some fine sarmons preached over the goods on a Sunday morning, seeing as how there was allus a grand muster of church folk mornin' arter a run. Ah! 'twas a werry 'spectable calling back-along. 'Tis surprising how things come back to one as one gets yarning. I mind when I was a pit of a nipper, mother used to teach us hymns of a Sunday afternoon. But the one I remember best was one old dad taught us, as we sat on his knee, 'Twas about a passon up Padstow way, time wrecking was allowed back-along. Well, one Sunday morning—leastways that's what old dad used to say, a ship got on to the Gull Rock while the folk was at church, and old Ephraim Blowey—that was the sexton, having been bred to the sea, always kept his weather eye liftin' seawards, and twigged it in a moment, and shouts, "Wreck!" and the congregation was on their feet in a jiffy. But the passon, being a conscientious man and werry strict about doing things right and proper, was all for fairplay—

Stop! stop! cried he, at least one prayer,
Let me get down, and all start fair.

I did hear that was one of Wesley's favourites.

P. R.—Right you are, old man; but the quality's changed since them days, sure 'nuff. They was werry merciful to the poor in times back. Aye, and werry sorry they was when a misfortinate chap came before them when they was sitting on the binch up at th' Court House, brought by them rascally 'Cisemen. Why, I've known them pay the fine themselves rather than see a chap locked up for carrying a drop of liquor. Certainly, they was werry merciful to the traders, and it was natural, seeing as how they couldn't get along without 'em. 'Spectable, do ye call it? If 'twasn't, why I'm dashed if I know what it was!

Capt. S.—And yet I can mind there was folk as said 'twas a

E

wrong thing to do—they called it chatin' the Govinment. Chatin' the Govinment, indeed! as if the Govinment warn't werry well able to take care of itsel. Aye, and what's more——

Z. K.—Axing your pardon, Mister, but the mention of churches set my brain-box working, and I was gwoin to ask the Cap'n yonder if it's true what they say 'bout Duloe Church—as how the folk kept piling in the tubs on the starboard side, 'cos 'twas handiest comin' up from the shore, 'till the foundations of the tower sunk so that they had to take 'en down, and build 'en up again at the expense of th' parish? You see, the tower got skew-wise, and like as if 'twould fall. Now, me'be, some on ye will have heard tell that afore, axin' your pardin for disturbing the flow o' conversation.

Capt. S.—Ees, old man, I reckon that's so.

P. R.—Well, to continny, there was folk time and again as would make believe they had a tweak of conscience when they was dying, and say they must get their minds aisy afore they left the flesh; though to my mind a chap orter have his conscience under better control than that. 'Tain't the time for reckoning up and striking a balance when you're on the slipways of the next world. A chap's brains ain't in no sort of order for figuring then. What he's done he must bide by—as you've made your bed so you mun lie on it. 'Tain't no time to repent when you can do nothing but lie still. But there's lots on 'em tries on that sort o' game. You'll have heard tell of Squire Hawkins, of Grampound. A power of trade used go pass through there back-along. He died me'be more nor a hundred year ago. Now, what did he do? Why, I'm darned if he didn't leave £600 to the King's Government— £600! think of that—to square up for what his tenants had chated the revenue of, so he said. Now, what do ye think of that? Was there iver sich a piece of fool's work? Why, his childers ought to have locked 'en up afore he put pen to paper. Ah, that writin' was the ruin o' lots of 'em. The only time a man orter put pen into ink is when he's giving a receipt for money paid. Look at Squire Hawkins, chating his childer out of their dues. Oh, 'twas a rascally business!

J. C.—I reckon old Squire Hawkins warn't the only one as thought to buy a free pass to Paradise by giving away what wasn't his'n, when he couldn't spend it no longer hissel. There was my old uncle Trenarren—him they called Wackem—you'll mind him, Dan? ter'ble command of language he had. Well, now, what d'ye think he did? He waur a free liver as you know. Aye, he lived every minute of his life, as they say. Well, just afore he went underground, and the family was reckoning they'd be a bit better off in an hour or two, what did he do? Why, shake me, if he didn't send off to St. Ossel for lawyer B——. Lord, how my memory do fail. I mean him they called Skin-'em-alive-o; and when he came he says—that's old uncle Trenarren—he says "I've been a sinful liver, Mr. B——, and cheated the King out of a ter'ble lot of stuff, and the only way I can aise my mind is by leaving my goods to the Lord." When we heard that we knewed what was coming, and brother Sam was for pitching old Skin-'em-alive-o out of the window; but the rest says, "Don't ee meddle wi' t' lawyer chap, or there be the divle to pay and no pitch hot." Well, the long and the shot of it was the old man signed away all to "good works," as he called them, 'cept a measley fifty pun. There warn't many of 'em as went to see 'en put under when the burrying came off, you bet! Now, d'ye mean to tell me that"l buy 'en a free pass to Paradise? No, not wi' stolen money, for I calls it stolen money when a man leaves it away from them to whom it rightly belongs. What's more, I tell ee whenever I sees in th' paper about a man dying and laving his chink to "good works" I says, depend on it that chap lived a merry life, and now he reckons to pave the road to heaven with guineas by chating his childers. No; what I says is this: Let a man give while he can enjoy hissel, and has to stint hissel to give; but when he's laid a-bed, all ready for going aloft, why, let others do the spending. Ain't that 'cording to Bible teaching?

J. S.—Well, vriends, as to the 'spectability of the trade, I think, seeing as how 'twas under the patronage of the gintry, to say nothing of church and chapel, we may take it as proved. 'Deed, 'twas a werry proper occipation for a self-respectin' man.

Why, dash it, where's Cap'n Stockem, and Tom, and the rest on 'em? Reckon they've slipped round to the King of Prewsia, and I'm danged if I ain't a bit dry mysel. So long, old man!

EDITOR'S NOTE.

The "Minutes of Proceedings" of the "Polruan Mutual Improvement Society, Ltd.," come to an abrupt end just here, and it would appear, from some rather confused and half-obliterated notes, that the meetings were adjourned *sine die* to enable Capt. Stockhollum, Literary Adviser to the Society, to conduct some further researches.

ENGLISH LAW AND CORNISH JURIES.

"A fellow-feeling makes us wondrous kind."
—*Garrick.*

TRIAL BY JURY.

≋

Was'ee up to Bodmin, time of th' 'Sizes, Mister Pascoe?

Why, surely, Mr. Julian, I waur on the Jury.

Aw, was ye now! Why, then, I reckon ye've somethin' to be proud on for the rest o' your days. Aye, and your childers arter you. 'Twas a Christian act getting that pore fellow clear of the law's grip, with they Lunnon chaps all dead agin him. But I reckon ye was one too many for 'en—they didn't know that a Cornish Jury warn't to be suborned; no, nor horrified wi' the sight of a wig. I should ha' been proud on't if I'd been ane on 'em.

Aye, you'm right, Mister Julian; but Lord, we had a ter'ble hard fight to get 'en clear, pore chap.

What did 'en try 'en for, Mister Pascoe?

Try 'en? Why, for felony.

Aye, but what had 'en done?

Done? Nothin' but tip over a Prewentive chap.

What! Did 'en try 'en for that?

Aye, that 'en did; 'twas the rascaliest business I've heard tell of for a long while. What else did they 'spect a man to do when one of they Prewentive chaps tried to rob him of his goods, what he'd bought and paid for, mind ye. I say, what could en do but tip 'en over?

But 'twas 'gin the law tapping 'en over the head, I reckon.

Aginst the law, d'ye say? Hang the law, says I; aye, and hang them as made the law what'd punish a pore fellow for defending his property from they land sharks. No; 'twarn't likely we'd find a chap guilty for doing same as we'd a-done oursels. 'Sides, I've a-knowed old Tom Couch all my life—a nice 'spectable fellow he is, too, baring it is when he gets a drop too much of sperrits into him. No; 'twasn't likely I'd be one to send him to a man-of-war for five years. But we had a ter'ble hard job to get 'en free.

'Twasn't all plain sailing, then?

No, 'twarn't. Why, you see, there was a chap from Padstow way—aye, a hard man he waur—he held out agin the rest of us, saying as how we mun abide by the law, aye, even if 'twas to hang 'en. Sich talk! I says to 'en, "We ain't bound by the law they Lunnon chaps brings down along wi' them, we'em a low to oursels here, I reckon. Let 'en try 'en by our ain laws—that's justice, not Lunnon laws." Oh, I tell ee, he was ter'ble stubborn, but there's an end to all things, if ye wait long enough. Well, we sat argifying till a quarter-less-twelve of the clock, when he says, looking at his watch—the Padstow chap, I mean—he says, "Well, I've done my dooty, I reckon, so well as I'm able, but as you'm all made up your minds to let the chap off, and seeing as how there's goods to be landed down at the Pill at three o'clock, me'be ten mile off, I must be 'tending to business, so ye may tell the Judge we'em agreed on the werdict—'tain't no good one setting hissel against twelve, that's a majolity enough to fix 'en. I'm a marciful man, but as 'twas aginst the law tapping that 'Ciseman chap over the nut, I'm thinking 'twould be as well to tell 'en—Tom, I mean—not to do it again, or me'be it'll go harder wi' 'en next time.

Reckon we can't do that, Mister—guilty or not guilty, that's the werdict; no 'twixt and between, I reckon.

Well, says the Padstow man, I've no but two hour to spare, so I 'spose I mun fall in with the majority; but, mind ye, 'twas agin the law all the same.

D—— the law, says the foreman—guilty or not guilty?

Not guilty.

You'm a Christian man, says I, tapping him on the shoulder. I reckon it'd have laid on your mind at the end if you'd knuckled under to they Lunnon folk. And with that the werdict was read out, and there was a ter'ble lot of cheering outside, for they was all dead agin the Lunnon folk.

WHERE THE CORNISHMEN FOUND
THEIR GOOD SPIRITS.

≋

"It is impossible totally to prevent smuggling; all that the Legislature can do is to compromise with a crime which, whatever laws may be made to constitute it a high offence, the mind of man can never conceive as at all equalling in turpitude those acts which are breaches of clear, moral virtues."—Lord Holland's speech in the House of Lords, July 9, 1805.

———

"We looked upon ourselves as peaceable and 'spectable traders."—"Confessions of a Smuggler."

ROSCOFF : A FAMOUS SMUGGLING ENTREPÔT.

≋

The Onion-boys—A once famous port—Saints from Cornwall—
Royal visitors—The two Trevanions—An insignificant ham-
let—How Roscoff grew rich—Cornish venturers—Where's
Roscoff?—Those mysterious cellars—The Smuggler-Evan-
gelist—Self-help—A sad New Year's Eve—Local history—
Some famous Merchants—The Cellars again—Small for-
tunes—Turning an honest penny—Paying for the spirits—
Madame S.—The clang of the Wooden Shoon—Where were
the Cruisers?—A ruse de guerre—The rejuvenescence of
Roscoff—Early vegetables—An inexhaustible Gold Mine—
A link with the past.

———

It is likely enough that the reader, in his peregrinations
over the land, has encountered certain blue-bloused folk of
foreign aspect festooned with onions. And if curiosity has
prompted him to interrogate these aliens he will have learnt that
they hail from a place called Roscoff—a piece of information, I
take it, which will not have conveyed very much, seeing that this
once famed port is not deemed important enough nowadays to
figure in school geography books. Though there was a time—
not so very remote, either—when the name would have touched
a sympathetic chord in most west-country households. And
thereby hangs a tale.

And first, let it be explained that this town, with a Russian-
sounding name, lies on the north coast of Brittany, vis-a-vis of
Cornwall, and may be more precisely located by drawing a line

due south from Plymouth across the Channel. Roscoff,* in fact, is the nearest French port to the Cornish shore; its position, in the centre of a circle whose circumference touches the Lizard on the one hand, and the Start on the other, supplying a clue to many curious circumstances in the history of its relations with the opposite coast.

Curiously enough, the earliest mention of Roscoff is in connection with a Saint—St. Pol or Paul—who, tradition affirms, crossed from Cornwall, a noted depot for saints in former ages, about the year 530, and founded a monastery on the adjacent island of Bas.

It was at Roscoff, too, many centuries later, that Mary, Queen of Scots landed, when only five years old, to be married to the Dauphin of France. The chapel of St. Ninian, now a ruin, was built as a memorial of her visit. There is a tradition, moreover, that the outline of her foot was cut on the rock where she first stepped ashore.

Even more romantic were the circumstances attending the visit of another Royal personage—the Pretender—who landed here after his adventurous escape from Scotland. The house wherein he lodged is still shewn.

Curious evidence of the long-standing connection between the Britons on either side of the Channel was afforded, moreover, on the landing of a batch of French prisoners-of-war at Falmouth, early in the 19th century, when, in answer to the roll-call, a Breton gave his name as Jean Trevanion de Carhayes, there being at the moment a Carhayes within a few miles of Falmouth owned by another John Trevanion.

The particular epoch in the history of Roscoff which concerns us here, however, opened about the middle of the 14th

---

*Cornishmen of a former generation always called the place "Rusco." And it is singular to find this rendering of the word in old documents. Thus, in a letter from Morlaix, dated May 15, 1586, we read of a "ship from Rusco." And in another from Sir Francis Drake to Queen Elizabeth, dated April 28, 1587, mention is made of "Rosco."

century, and was brought about in this wise. The British Government, after nearly fifty years of expostulation with the authorities of the Channel Islands for their tacit encouragement of the smuggling trade, at last put their foot down, and established Custom-houses in the Islands. Commenting on this arbitrary interference with trade customs, the historian of Guernsey writes :—" The object of the British Government in framing this restrictive Act (1767) was evidently to protect her own revenue by putting a check to smuggling; but the scheme was not as successful as anticipated. High duties will operate as a bounty and encouragement to illicit trade, and if one opening be stopped another will soon be discovered. Thus it happened with the attempt of the British Government to secure its revenues by depriving the Channel Islands of their chartered rights. A large share of the illicit trade was transferred to Roscoff, a small village on the coast of Brittany. This insignificant hamlet immediately became an interesting object to the French Government, and it is worthy of note that no sooner were the officers of Customs established in Guernsey and Jersey than the question of making Roscoff a free port or *port d'entrepôt* was discussed in the French Councils and immediately agreed to. Its effect was soon felt. Roscoff, till then an unknown and unfrequented port, the resort only of a few fishermen, rapidly grew into importance, so that from small hovels it soon possessed commodious houses and large stores, occupied by English, Scotch, Irish, and Guernsey merchants.* These, on the one hand, gave every incentive to the British smugglers to resort there, and on the other hand the French Government afforded encouragement to the merchants."

And thus was inaugurated an era of extraordinary prosperity for the " insignificant hamlet." And for fifty years or more the dialects of Scotland, Ireland, and the West-country must have

---

*The " Cruel Coppinger " of Mr. Hawker's " Footprints of former men in Far Cornwall," and of Mr. Baring Gould's " In the Roar of the Sea," is said to have been an Irish squire who bought property at Roscoff, which was lost, however, in the Revolution of 1792.

seemed almost as familiar to the natives of Roscoff as their own
mother tongue. Cornishmen, especially, flocked to this port, at
all seasons of the year, oft-times crossing in small open boats at
great personal risk in the pursuit of illicit gain. This was the
golden age of Roscoff.

Some faint conception of the volume of commerce that
flowed from this small port into British homes may be gathered
from the official records for March, 1832. Thus, in a letter to
the Customs authorities in London, a " well-informed correspondent " writes from Roscoff:—" Smuggling has not been carried
on here so extensively at any time during the last twenty years as
it is now." And he gives the following list of sailings and
arrivals:—

Arrivals between March 13th and 31st—

Goldfinch	14 tons	from	Plymouth.
Four Brothers	12 ,,	,,	Plymouth.
Goldfinch	17 ,,	,,	Dartmouth.
Supply	9 ,,	,,	Dartmouth.
Rose	13 ,,	,,	Lizard.
Dove	18 ,,	,,	Cowes.
Eagle	35 ,,	,,	Fowey.
William	13 ,,	,,	Falmouth.
Love	26 ,,	,,	Coverack.
Goldfinch (2nd trip)	14 ,,	,,	Plymouth.
Eagle (2nd trip)	35 ,,	,,	Fowey.
Love (2nd trip)	26 ,,	,,	Coverack.

Departures between March 15th and 27th.

*Goldfinch	with 90 tubs	for	Plymouth.
Four Brothers	,, 20 ,,	,,	Plymouth.
Goldfinch	,, 120 ,,	,,	Dartmouth.
Supply	,, 60 ,,	,,	Dartmouth.
Rose	,, 80 ,,	,,	Lizard.
Dove	,, 125 ,,	,,	Cowes.
*Eagle	,, 150 ,,	,,	Fowey.
*Love	,, 125 ,,	,,	Coverack.
William	,, 80 ,,	,,	Falmouth.

NOTE.—The three boats marked (*) have been very successful,
especially the last, on board which are the two Dunstans. They
sailed on the 27th, landed their cargoes, and were back at Roscoff
on the 31st.

As years rolled by, reductions in the spirit duties at home
diminished the smugglers' profits; the visits of Cornishmen be-

came less frequent, and the golden harvest of the Ruscovites was proportionately reduced. With the fifties smuggling practically ceased, and, once again, so far as Cornishmen were concerned, the little Brittany town became an "unknown and unfrequented port," in proof of which may be cited the significant fact that, at the present time, not one native of the Duchy out of a hundred can spot the position of Roscoff on the map, a circumstance which seems to imply a shocking indifference to one of the most eventful chapters of county history, if not a grave defect in Duchy educational methods. Think of folk attaining to years of discretion without acquiring even the most rudimentary knowledge of a business which engrossed the time and energy of their forbears!—growing up in ignorance of the very names of the enterprising fellows who conducted a great industry in times past! What would the men of Wesley's day have thought of a generation of Cornishmen, aye, and women, too, who knew not how to sink and work a crop of goods; nay, who were unable even to tell a tub of spirits from a beer barrel? Degeneracy has, indeed, set in!

The ignorance of strangers concerning the useful *rôle* which Roscoff once filled in the economy of Cornish households is less surprising. Even so versatile a writer as Charles Wood, in describing a visit to this Breton port, omits all mention of its commercial associations. Though what he does say amply confirms the statement as to its decadence. " Few scenes in Brittany," he writes, " are more characteristic and impressive than this little-known town; the streets are deadly and deserted; never yet, in Brittany, had we felt so out of the world and removed from civilization."

Once only, and then quite unwittingly, does this writer bring us into touch with the vanished past. " Its quaint houses are substantially built, and many of them still possess the old cellars that open by large doors into the streets; the cellars go far back, and light never penetrates into their recesses." But why not tell us, Mr. Wood, the purpose for which these cellars were excavated? For thereby hangs an interesting story.

The further allusion to a certain "stone pier" recalls some touching, albeit long-forgotten, associations of a widely different nature. For it was on this identical pier, during the last quarter of the 18th century, when the smuggling trade was in full swing, that Captain Harry Carter, smuggler and evangelist, conducted his Sunday afternoon Services for the benefit of the gentle souls engaged in that exciting business. This strange blend of saint and sinner—a product which seems to have been indigenous to the "delectable Duchy"—took to smuggling very early in life, and one gathers from his autobiography that he was blest with a tender and enlightened conscience, and earnestly strove to raise the tone of the smuggling service, seeing that, at the age of 18, when he was already in command of a smuggler, he made a law on board against swearing "under pain of punishment."

At the age of thirty the worthy captain would seem to have experienced a second and more convincing "call," for it was then he started his Evangelistic Services on the pier at Roscoff. On one occasion, he tells us in his autobiography, the congregation —some twenty or thirty—comprised "all the Englishmen in the town, who took off their hats and set themselves down." While another time, three large cutters from Guernsey arriving, their captains and several of the men came to attend service at his house—"all very serious, no laffing, no trifling conversations," a pattern to many congregations at home. And so on. One can only hope that the good seed bore fruit, in spite of the unpromising soil.

Meanwhile, acting on the principle that "Heaven helps those who help themselves," the worthy captain neglected none of the material means for bringing his enterprises to a successful issue. Such entries in the diary as the following show with what excellent judgment the affairs of this world were conducted :—"Bought a cutter of 60 tons and 19 guns ;" and, again, "a new lugger of 20 tons." Nevertheless, as there is "no rose without a thorn," so, in spite of a trust in Providence, backed up with guns and small arms, things sometime went awry, as witness the fate of "a lugger of 45 tons with 16 carriage guns" surprised by two man-of-war boats on the night of January 30, 1788, while landing in Costan (query Cawsand). And though, by God's mercy, the skipper escaped, he must have spent a rather depressing New Year's Eve. On the other hand, the Government paid him the compliment of offering a reward of £300 for his capture.*

But the scraps of local lore vouchsafed by the Smuggler-Evangelist are not entirely satisfying, and so the present writer, with a view to improving his own knowledge, placed himself in communication with an esteemed inhabitant of Roscoff who, he was assured, knew more about the place than most people. The reply was prompt and courteous, and the following extracts from a mass of curious information placed at the writer's disposal will, he feels sure, interest the public :—

" Beyond what I now enclose no history of Roscoff exists, nor of its commerce, nor of its splendour in the last century. In the papers belonging to the old houses I have found little. Previous to the last century its traditions speak with terror of the incursions of the English, and the fights which took place on the coasts. Queen Mary Stewart took refuge here, as you are aware, and everything points to the conclusion that all the preparations for the voyage here were made by her countrymen resident in Roscoff.

" During the latter part of the 18th century privateering found here a good base of operations; and during the continental blockade, under Napoleon, tobacco was very scarce and dear in France, just as brandy was in England. The French Government permitted brandy to be exported, but confiscated tobacco and salt unsparingly, imposing the most formidable penalties, and this so arbitrarily, that the rich adventurers, with three or four exceptions, died in poverty; and little by little Roscoff fell into the precarious state in which it has remained since the first half of this century.

---

*See " The Autobiography of a Cornish Smuggler," by John B. Cornish, 1900.

F

"Several of the old houses have subterranean passages, and very deep cellars. The earliest owners of these houses had English names, such as "McCulloch,"* "Greenlaw," etc. The latter was owner of the house in which I live, and which was built in 1654-1771. The name has been Frenchified into 'Sieur de Verte Loi.' Some of the houses of that period, built of granite, and more or less altered by repairs, have lost their venerable aspect.

"This little place had certainly a brilliant commercial period. The trade which was carried on between Roscoff and the south coast of England, from 1815 to 1840, consisted of brandy from this shore, and tobacco from the other side: the French exporting brandy into Great Britain by smuggling, and the English from Plymouth, and that neighbourhood repaying them in tobacco and money.

"Long before the date already named, this trade had existed, according to old documents, as far back as 1763; but from 1815 to 1840 the trade was very considerable. The firms of Malabee and de'Lisle, and others of less importance, made a wholesale business of it. Several times they had to pay heavy fines, the ships and cargoes were captured, and the crews imprisoned in the prisons and hulks at Portsmouth and Plymouth. If much was to be gained by the trade, the risks were certainly considerable.

"The establishments here have ceased to exist for a long time; the sheds and underground warehouses to which the goods were conveyed had doors that opened on to the sea, so that at high tide the boats passed loaded into the sheds. Once the boats were inside, the Custom-house authorities had no right to visit these warehouses, although they knew smuggled goods were there. The new law, made in 1840, permitted domiciliary

---

*Captain Harry Carter, the smuggler, frequently mentions a family of this name from whom he received much kindness at the time of the Revolution. The family afterwards migrated to Guernsey, where some of the descendants are still living.

visits, and a double watch being at the same time exercised on the English coasts, put an end to this smuggling trade.

"Malabee, Wege, and Bagot made small fortunes in the trade, and descendants of these families are still in Roscoff, and very much respected. I myself live in one of the sheds used for hiding the boats on returning from England with tobacco. I have made a chalet of it. I have also bought Bagot's property, where are large cellars used for preparing the brandy for export— these places are well worth a visit."

It is to be noted that the law of 1840, while affecting the importation of tobacco into France, and thus hampering the free interchange of commodities with the English smugglers, in no wise interfered with the export of brandy. British smuggling boats, therefore, continued to resort to Roscoff as heretofore.

In the Customs' records of this date frequent mention is made of Irish agents at Roscoff, as also of the merchants "Mallaby," "de'Lisle," etc. From these documents it further appears that, in July, 1830, a notification was issued to the Coastguard stations to the effect that "the French Government having lately conceded to the ports of Morlaix and Roscoff the privilege of exporting tobacco and snuff in small packages, with a view to encouraging British and Irish smugglers to resort thither; in consequence of this measure, two French travellers have passed through Guernsey on their way to Ireland for the avowed purpose of organizing operations."

On reading the above remarks to an old smuggling acquaintance—a well-known character—who in his day had made many a trip to Roscoff, and boasted a profound acquaintance with the ins and outs of the trade, the old man evinced the liveliest interest. He said the names of the merchants were perfectly familiar to him; but he strongly objected to the mention of "small fortunes" being made out of the business—"small fortunes, indeed! Why, they must have made thousands of pounds: they were sending away at least a thousand tubs a week!" was the old man's comment. Some of his further remarks are worth quoting.

"What you read out about the tobacco smuggling into France is quite true; but it was brought from Jersey, not England. The Plymouth chaps mostly used to get the tobacco, and exchange it with the merchants at Roscoff for spirits. You see there were no duties in the Channel Islands, that was why tobacco was so cheap there. But besides tobacco, it was a common thing to take nick-nacks over to sell, and then to pay for the spirits with the proceeds. For instance, I took over an anvil one trip and sold it for £7—it only cost me £3 in England. Then you could buy needles in England for a penny or twopence a dozen, and sell them in France for a franc. White stockings, again, would cost you a shilling the pair, and fetch five francs at Roscoff. Files, too, costing threepence, would fetch a franc and a half. We could make a lot of money in that way, you see, and pay for the liquor we bought. We made just as much coming back as we did going there; for instance, tea could be bought at Roscoff for tenpence which would cost eight or nine shillings a pound in England. Salt, again, which was fivepence a pound, would only cost about three halfpence in France. That was how we used to manage things."

My old smuggler friend further informed me that sometimes there were as many as twenty or thirty Englishmen over at Roscoff, "and a jolly lot of fellows they were, too, and up to any lark—not mischief—mind you. Oh, no! we never did any harm to anyone, but we used to have some rare games. There was Madame S——, I remember her well; she kept a great hotel—like the one up at Fowey, where we always put up—I wonder if she is living still? She would be about the same age as I am. She was a fine woman, I can tell you; and, what's more, she had some fine daughters—nice, decent young women, they were, too —I suppose they'll all be married now? The time I'm speaking of was about 1832.

"One time I was over there," continued the old man, "the cholera was raging terrible bad, and over one hundred people died in a week. There was nothing but the pattering of wooden clogs along the street, after the dead, all day long. None of the

English caught it, though fifteen of us were over there at the time."

It must not be supposed, however, from the energy with which the smuggling trade was carried on, that the Revenue cruisers were inactive.

The following extract from an old Order Book gives some idea of what went on :—" In consequence of several well-known smuggling boats being absent from Cawsand, and supposed to be taking in cargoes at Roscoff, the Revenue cutter Harpy, of the Plymouth station, was sent across to look them up, and, on re-connoitering outside Roscoff, discovered there the Little Henry, of Portsmouth ; the Bee, Jane, and Friend's Endeavour, of Cawsand ; and the Hope, of Polperro." There is a note appended to the effect that " these boats being outside of their limits are liable to seizure on attempting to return to the English coast."

The sequel may be gathered from a later entry :—" In consequence of the large number of Cawsand and other English boats that have been recently taken, lost, or made to throw overboard their cargoes, the Coastguards are warned of the probability of the smugglers employing French boats to bring over their cargoes."

The expedient of employing French vessels enabled smuggling to be carried on with varying success for some time longer. But every year the preventive chain was being tightened, while large reductions in the import duties at length reduced the profits of the business to the vanishing point, and with the extinction of smuggling the link which had bound Roscoff to Great Britain for so long a period was snapped asunder.

And now, strange to say, after an interval of nearly fifty years, commercial intercourse between Roscoff and the British Islands is being revived, and a tide of prosperity has set in, which, if taken at the flood, may lead to fortune. And this changed aspect of affairs has been brought about by the enterprise of the ubiquitous, blue-bloused onion-seller, who may be regarded as the outward and visible sign of the new era which has dawned on the Breton port.

The revival of trade is thus explained by a recent visitor :—
" Roscoff itself is extremely fertile—the dead aspect of the little
town does not extend to the surrounding plains. The climate is
much influenced by the Gulf Stream, and the winters are temper-
ate. Flowers and vegetables grow here all the year round that
in less favoured districts are found only in the summer. Like
Provence, in the far south, Roscoff is famous for its " primeurs,"
or early vegetables."

We learn from a Consular report that, from Roscoff, in a
single year twenty-six different companies, composed of over
four hundred members, visited the following ports in the United
Kingdom for the purpose of selling their garden produce :—Jersey, Guernsey, Portsmouth, Weymouth, Exeter, Plymouth, Falmouth, Swansea, Newport, Portmadoc, Bangor, Liverpool, New-
castle, Glasgow, and Greenock. From these ports they extend
their operations in all directions ; for instance, taking Newport
as a centre, one party will go inland by rail for a distance of one
hundred miles, returning to headquarters every Saturday night ;
while others, in parties of four, go about the country with a
handcart, returning to Newport every night.

Nor are the French authorities neglectful of this new found
source of wealth. The Secretary to the Society of Agriculture
for the Department of Finisterre, for example, some time ago
made an earnest appeal to other districts to follow the good example set by the people of Roscoff, and go forth and offer from
door to door, both in France and in England, their butter,
cheese, and other produce.

These enterprising pedlars may now be met with in all parts
of the United Kingdom. The present writer has seen and con-
versed with them in English, Welsh, and Irish towns, and even
in Keswick. And from an intelligent young man who spoke good
English the following facts were elicited :—" There are too
many people living in Roscoff to be able to earn a living, and
so we are obliged to travel about in search of work. At least ꞁ
thousand Roscoff men come over to England every year to sell
vegetables, so that, in fact, scarcely anyone is left at home except

the old people." This young man, though but 24 years of age, had visited most parts of the world. The vessel he had crossed in remained at Cardiff; but the depot was at Bridgend, where he slept every night. Four brothers-in-law had come over with him, and they would remain in England for about four months, until the stock was sold out. On returning to Roscoff they would have to go to sea for the winter.

Apropos, an interesting letter from the French Rear Admiral Reveillere appeared in the "Journal des Economistes" (Nov. 15, 1902), in which, after explaining that for three years past he had commanded the Ecole de Pilotage on the north coast of France, this distinguished officer stated that recently a number of onion shippers who had just returned from England said to him, "You see, sir, there is a regular river of gold flowing over to us every day from England, and not a particle of our soil passes over there." And the Admiral went on to state that "during my three years' stay on this coast I have come to the profound conviction that England is, for the toilers of our coast, an inexhaustible gold mine; and I hold that the people who egg on others to a hatred of that excellent clientelle are engaged in a vile trade." And the Admiral proceeded to describe the reception accorded to the onion sellers across the Channel, notwithstanding the wholesale calumny practised against English people in France at the time of the South-African war. "We were not very proud at the beginning of the war," said a shipper to the Admiral, "but matters soon came right. Working men, above all, always made us welcome; and in Scotland we rarely conclude a bargain but we are invited to take a seat at the family table and made completely at home."

Strange, indeed, is the persistency with which trade adheres to old-established lines of communication. The newly-developed onion industry, for example, has kept to the route opened up in the first instance by the spirit smugglers. And many another once noted smuggling entrepot has become the centre of a new sort of commerce, which bids fair to rival, and, probably, far exceed the old one, both in volume and importance.

When, therefore, the reader next encounters the ubiquitous gentleman in the blue blouse he will, perchance, view him with more interest than heretofore, as forming a link with an eventful past and as the embodiment of an intercourse which has been maintained with scarcely a break for nearly four centuries.

"DEEP SIXTEEN"; OR, THE SMUGGLER'S DEATH.

SMUGGLER—" A wretch, who, in defiance of justice and the laws, imports or exports goods either contraband or without payment of the customs."—" Dictionary of the English Language," by Samuel Johnson, LL.D.

" A person who, though no doubt highly blamable for violating the laws of his country, is frequently incapable of violating those of natural justice, and would have been in every respect an excellent citizen had not the laws of his country made that a crime which nature never meant to be so."—Definition of a Smuggler, by Adam Smith.

"DEEP SIXTEEN"; OR, THE SMUGGLER'S DEATH.

≈≈≈≈≈≈

"He was a man, take him for all in all,
I shall not look upon his like again."
—"Hamlet."

"Yes, sir, he was werry much respected; and you'll not be surprised arter what I told you before. He stuck to his trade as long as he was able to go afloat; and when he got too old for that he took to lighter jobs—some on 'em takes to drink, but old dad being an edicated man cottoned on to his Bible, which was werry right and proper at his time of life. Yes, sir, every Sunday arternoon, as soon as dinner was stowed, and he'd had his pipe—and he was a most remarkable man for his wittals —as hearty an eater as ever I see'd—well, directly the old man got settled, mother'd bring out the family Bible, and before you could say knife the old chap had settled his head on to it, and would be snoring away like a steam hooter in a fog.

"Maybe you'll have heard, sir, as how the old man did a bit of free-trading in his day—'smuggling' they calls it now! Well, sir, afore he coiled his ropes up for a full-due, he used to go on a deal about that there Free-trade, saying as it was a wrong thing to do. 'Cos why? 'Cos there warnt no sort of sartinty about it. You never knew where you were—come to-day, gone to-morrow! Well, sure enough 'twas a falterin' sort of business, and I don't wonder the old man see'd the wickedness of it arter losing that last crop of goods down by Hemmick Cove, yonder. Aye, 'twas enough to conwart any man! Don't you think he was right, sir, to turn round on it arter being sarved so?"

" It would have been better if he'd seen the wrong of it a little sooner, in my opinion."

" Why, sir, you wouldn't have had him show the white feather while the luck was with him?"

" There'd have been all the more merit in it then!"

" Well, 'taint no good argifying with an unreasonable man like yourself—begging your pardon, sir! Howsumever, we ain't all run in the same mould; and as old dad was a werry religious man, I take it, what he did was according to regulations. But what I was a-going to say was this, there was a wast of uncertainty about it. Look at the bitter times we had coming back from Rusco—in the winter season—the month of March was as bad as any for crossing, seeing 'twas a faltering time—calm one day, blowing fit to tear a sow's ear off the next. Why, now, there was the werry last time old dad and me crossed together; that was afore he saw the wickedness of it. There was Uncle Ben, and Tom Dunstan—Sweety, we called him—and another chap. . . . Lord, how my memory does fail (scratching his head), but no matter—he war a sarcy chap, though. Well, we'd hardly got clear of the Isle of Bass—may be you'll have been to Rusco, sir? No!—we began to make for Easting. You see, the ebb was running werry strong, and there was every sign of wind from the east'ard—wild looking sky, it was, to be sure— air nippy, too. Well, we'd laid her by the wind, under easy canvas, and were busy getting the sinking stones ready to bend on— the old man was werry particular about that, ever since that time he was caught on the ground hop, and had to heave over all of a hurry, and leave the tubs floating about like ducks on a pond. We was sorting out the stones, when Tom Dunstan—him we called Sweety—wonderful fine sight he had, to be sure—could tell a Prewentive wessel as soon as most chaps could make out the head of her tops'l. Well, the old man had been prying out to windward, and all of a sudden he calls out, ' Slam me if there aint the old Switchtail coming down afore the wind!' That was the old Fox, not the new Fox—the Revenue cutter stationed at Fowey. So we 'bout ship, and ran back under the Bass, waited there till dusk, and then stood across. The wind was freshening up all the time, and about eleven o'clock that night we cotched it strong—green seas breaking over us everywhere. Tom Dunstan—him as we called Sweety—was for putting the tubs out, but old' dad said no, hang on a bit. She was labouring ter'able— you see, we was choke full of tubs, and low in the water. At last we shipped a sea which pretty nigh swamped us, and then old dad says, 'We'm no help for it; out with 'em!' Most of the tubs was bent on by this time, and so we down jib, ran her up in the wind, and began to pay out the drift line with the tubs bent on. Directly they were all out we down canvas, and lay by the tubs all night. The vessel lay easy enough, though, of course, she drifted a deal to leeward, but that was better than losing tubs and wessel! We was pretty nigh froze afore the morning, for you see we was wet through, and the craft had taken in such a power of water we couldn't get a fire lit in the bit of a f'xsl. It was sleet and snow, too, all the time. Well, the breeze soon blowed itself out. We picked up the tubs, got canvas on her, and next evening ran in by Mousehole and sunk the goods on safe ground, and got good bearings. Time we got in to Penzance we was that stiff with cold we could hardly finger the canvas. Now, that'll give you an idea of the sort of work it was—aye, bitter times we had, and no mistake; and when we lost the goods into the bargain; why, there's no wonder sum on 'em was brought to see the wickedness of it!

"Well, sir, to continny. I was telling you as how old dad, being an edicated man, took to his Bible when he got too old for going afloat. Oh, he was werry religious, though, to be sure, there was some said as he lived his life when he was young—he lived to be a werry old man, as you may know, sir—89 years four months three days—that was his age afore he slipped his moorings. As I was saying, the old man couldn't get along of a Sunday afternoon without the family Bible. Arter he'd had his bit nap he'd turn over till he got to the Hactses, and run his finger along till he come to the official log of that there craft what St. Paul shipped aboard of, time he was wrecked at Malta—druv on the lee shore there. The old boy was werry fond of seafaring matters, and he'd finger away over that there log of the grain ship what belonged to Alexandria till the print was pretty nigh all rubbed away. He'd spin a fine yarn to the youngsters about what he'd a-done supposing as how he'd been aboard that there craft; for, you see, he'd sailed the Mediterranean in his day, and knew the winds to a haffygraphy; and, to tell you the truth, he thought precious small beer of them Egyptians or Greeks, or whatever they was as signed articles aboard that craft. He used to say he'd been shipmates along of some Greeks, and he reckoned them about as mutinous a lot as ever he sailed with, and no account as seamen neither. For my part, I never could understand how them corn ships, as they called them, came to be lading grain at Alexandria; all the wessels I've ever come across as sailed in tha trade shipped grain in the Black Sea—Odessa way. But I s'pose them furriners trades different to us. Is that so, sir?

"There was one thing old dad never did believe in, that there 'undergirding,' as they called it. He used to say he couldn't understand however the Board of Trade Inspector ever came to let such a ramshackle old craft put to sea—unless he'd been squared—and with a shipload of passengers, too; although they was but a lot of sojers and conwicts. Still, they was men. May be you know, sir, there's nothing so dangerous as a leaky ship. If the water gets amongst the corn it's sure to bust out her sides, undergirding or no undergirding. P'raps they wasn't as strict in them days as they are now? No Plimsoll-mark, I reckon?

"'Twas a rum go, too, to my mind, putting to sea with such a passul of longshore chaps and beachcombers as they had for a crew. Got into the hands of some rascally shipping agent, I suppose? 'Twas like 'em, too, sneaking off in the boat, all on the sly, when the wessel was on the rocks. Chaps what'll do that sort of thing ought to be strung up, to my mind. I've heard some people say that the military orficer aboard oughter have listened to what Paul told him, and laid up the old craft for the winter. But was it likely he'd pay more attention to a conwict than the skipper? No, 't'warnt likely!

"Old dad used to think a lot of that there Paul, though, to be sure, he warn't bred to the sea. But, mind you, he never blamed the sojer orficer—centurion, or whatever they called him —for not taking his advice; it didn't seem natural that a shore-going chap would make a better forecast than a man trained to the sea! But, as I was telling you, the old man used to say Paul was about the only chap aboard that there craft as kept his head in the breeze of wind—aye, and wasn't off his feed, either! 'Twas like they furriners eating nothing for fourteen days! To my mind it was a queer thing how they could work without vittals. Anyways, it put heart into them when they did have a bite and a sup, for they turned to and huv out all the wheat.

"They made a werry pretty landfall, too, considering as how they never steered no course, but let the craft drift. It was ten to one the wessel didn't go bang up agin the cliffs—wild place to chance on in a gale of wind, that there island. Been to Malta, I s'pose, sir? Bus'lin' place they tell me; anyways, there'll be more going on in the Grand Harbour now in a day than there was in a year time we reads about, I reckon. No steamers then, I s'pose?

"Well, the old man used to run on, calling the soundings and checking 'em off on an old chart he'd picked up sumveres, and plotting out the wessel's track arter she left the Fair Havens. And by the time he'd got her into broken water he mostly dozed off, with his 'ead on the book; and mother used to say, if he'd as much larnin' inside his old nut as he had underneath it he'd 'a been a cleverer man nor the passon. Anyways, it made a fine pillow for the old boy, and he mostly slept on till tea-time.

"The only thing what riled mother was when the old chap's pipe tumbled out of his mouth, and she had to nip it up sharp afore it burnt the Bible; though many's the time I've seen the ashes tumble out, and 'twas a wonder there never was a blaze-up! Sometimes she'd try and clap a hakerchief under his head, for he'd made the pages that greasy along o' his old nut it almost shined; but she had to do it werry gingerly, so as not to disturb the old boy, for he had a rough tongue if he was woke up sudden—had a trick of rapping out things as 'd startle you. He'd a surprisin' command of language, as you know, sir.

"I can see the old chap now, with his head on the book, and his pipe just a-going to fall. Oh, he was werry religious, sir —never missed a Sunday without his nap a-top of the family Bible. Why, the werry day he slipped his moorings he had the Bible brought up to his bed, and checked the soundings as he lay there. We was most of us about him, for the doctor said he didn't think he could last long. Mother had just brought him a sup of tea, when he called out, 'Deep sixteen,' and dropped off as quiet as a new-born infant.

"Yes, sir, them was the last words old dad ever spoke. He never said a word arter. And where do you think his finger lay, sir? He'd been fuddling away at the leaves till he'd lost his place, and when mother came to look his finger lay pointing at the words, 'The troubles of the righteous are werry great.' Yes, sir, that's where his finger lay, and mother had it marked off— you may see it in the book to this day! 'Twas a werry proper text, sir, I'm thinking, for, you see, the old man was werry religious, and he'd lived a hard life as ever a man had. Mother had the words cut on the old man's headstone, and you may see it up to Churchtown, in the corner, bearing about S.S.E. from the porch. He allus had a hankering arter that there billet; you see, it lay snug and quiet under the lee of the squire's vault. There's a grapnel cut on the stone, too, and a bit of tarred drift-line round the grave. Yes, sir, he lived by them when he was with us, and 'tis fitting they should be nigh his body now. (After a long pause) I've heard say, sir, there's to be no sea in the next world. Is that Gospel, sir?"

"So we're told, John."

"I'm thinking, then, the old chap'll be werry hard put for a job, for he never liked kicking his heels about on shore for long."

Lightning Source UK Ltd
Milton Keynes UK
UKOW021855140213

206319UK00005B/69/P